Introduction to
African American
Photographs
1840 - 1950
Identification, Research, Care & Collecting

Ross J. Kelbaugh

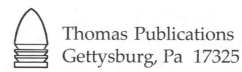

Thomas Publications
Gettysburg, Pa 17325

Title page photograph: Photo postcard of Beulah Feaster by the Flatbush Photo Studio, Brooklyn, NY, ca. 1915.

TABLE OF CONTENTS

Photographer Moorer from Philadelphia posed making a landscape photograph with his Kodak Folding Pocket Model 3A camera around 1915. The inexpensive photo postcards that could be printed from this camera's negative made photography available to many African Americans during the first decades of the 1900s.

INTRODUCTION

In recent years the vintage photographs of African Americans have received greater attention by historians, collectors, institutions and, most importantly, African American themselves. However, when examining recent publications that feature black photographs, it becomes readily apparent that there is still a need for help in the interpretation of this important historical resource. Though much has been written about the history of photography and numerous guides to photograph collecting exist, African American photographs are still being misinterpreted limiting their potential contribution to black history. This book has been written to help in the identification and dating of these visual artifacts, to provide recommendations for their research, and to offer some guidance for those interested in their collection and preservation.

I began collecting African American photographs back in the early 1970s as I sought out 19th century and early 20th century American images at antique shows, flea markets, antique shops, auctions, and vintage photography shows. Now competition among individual collectors and cultural institutions vying to make their collections more inclusive has caused rapidly escalating prices and new interest in preserving what was largely forgotten not so long ago. Hopefully, this book will help to further the appreciation and survival of our black visual legacy.

Most publications are made possible by the input of many who have shared their time, thoughts and effort. Sandra David was a great help in rediscovering the story of Elizabeth Fairfax. Gil Barrett, Henry Deeks, Mark Johnson, Howard McManus, and Gail Zlotowitz generously made several outstanding images available for publication. Unless otherwise noted, photographs are from my personal collection. Earl J. Coates, Sharon Spacco, and George Whiteley, IV provided invaluable editorial commentary. I would like to acknowledge my parents, Harry and Marjorie Kelbaugh, who instilled in me at an early age an appreciation for our nation's heritage. And I would like to make note of my maternal grandmother, Lilly Maye Sharp, who had the patience to show me all of the old family photographs when I was a fidgety twelve year old. As a lesson for us all, she knew the names of everyone on those cartes de visite, cabinet cards and large format family reunion photographs, only to have much of those identities lost because she did not write them down on the back before she passed away. Lastly, I would particularly like to thank my wife, Nancy, for her editorial help in shaping this publication and, most importantly, for giving me the initial idea for its creation.

Ross J. Kelbaugh
Baltimore, MD
www.HistoricGraphics.com

Focal Point: Frederick Douglass Sets Auction Record

Half-plate daguerreotype of Frederick Douglass taken by Samuel J. Miller in Akron, Ohio, in 1852. The spotting in the image is due to the decomposition of the period glass.

Courtesy of Mark Johnson

All collectors dream of finding "the big one" while on the hunt for antique treasures. A half-plate daguerreotype of an African American is among the biggest find to have been discovered in recent years.

In the spring of 1996, a Pittsburgh auction house advertised a sale that included a group of daguerreotype portraits of American Indians among the items to be sold. Several local photography collectors attended the preview with great interest drawn by their knowledge of the rarity of early images of Native Americans. Not mentioned in the newspaper ads for the auction were several other daguerreotypes whose importance was less obvious to the sellers.

As the photography collectors examined the items at the Friday night preview, they made an unbelievable discovery. In addition to the rare Indian daguerreotypes were two others that set emotions ablaze! Upon opening one of the quarter-plate cases, previewers saw the daguerreotype of a clean shaven abolitionist John Brown intensely confronting the camera's lens as he clutched the edge of a flag in one hand while raising his other as if he was swearing an oath. In addition, it was housed in a miniature case signed by the African American daguerreotypist Augustus Washington! This was a portrait that had been published in a book decades earlier and whose location had been lost. Then opening a half-plate case they saw the intense face of Frederick Douglass sternly looking back at them. This image also bore the imprint of the Akron, Ohio, daguerreotypist Samuel J. Miller embossed on the interior pad opposite the daguerreotype. The chances of such stunning discoveries being made at a local estate auction were incalculable. That evening, phone calls went out and coalitions were formed preparing for the showdown that would occur at the next day's auction.

The following Saturday morning the factions gathered eagerly anticipating the sale of these daguerrean gems. Eventually each lot came up and after spirited bidding between the representatives for two rival groups, one became the proud owners of John Brown's "lost" portrait and the other laid claim to Frederick Douglass's newly discovered plate. But their victories did not come cheap as each of the images sold in the low five figures. The saga, however, of these newly discovered daguerrean treasures did not end there.

In October 1996, the two daguerreotypes were placed in the annual fall photography sale at the renown auction house Sotheby's in New York. Full color reproductions pictured the two plates in the lavish catalog along with extensive descriptions about their history and importance. No accidental discoveries were going to be made this time. Much debate raged in the daguerrean community about which of the two would command the higher price and many experienced collectors believed that the Brown daguerreotype would receive the honors. After another round of heated bidding Frederick Douglass was once again sold, but this time for $184,000! A representative bidding for the Chicago Art Institute won the competition and the museum announced its acquisition officially as part of its Black History Month celebrations in February 1997. Following the sale of the Douglass plate, the daguerreotype of John Brown was bought by a photography dealer bidding for the National Portrait Gallery in Washington, D.C., for $129,000. It was an interesting coincidence of history that had brought the daguerreotypes of these two men together again. Their last meeting when alive forced Douglass to flee to Europe to escape the suspicions of his involvement in John Brown's raid at Harper's Ferry.

Perhaps you are now asking yourself why so much money was paid for these images, especially for one of a former slave that is not much larger than your hand. This book will help you answer that question as you are introduced to vintage photographic formats like daguerreotypes. It will also help you find out more about their subjects and the people who made them, how to care for these images, and give you tips on collecting them. Who knows what photographic treasures of black history are yet to be discovered?

Sixth-plate daguerreotype of an anonymous black girl taken by B.F. Tyler & Co. in New York around 1852. Her dress indicates that she was the daughter of a successful African American family who were among the more than 420,000 free blacks in the United States at that time. The daguerreotypist hand tinted the upholstery and dress as well as highlighted her jewelry. The girl had moved her fan during the exposure that lasted several seconds causing it to blur. Fine examples of daguerreotype portraits of free blacks are rare.

1

THE DAGUERREOTYPE

In 1839, the first widespread photographic medium became available to the world. Named the daguerreotype after its French discoverer, Louis Daguerre, it quickly spread to the United States and by September 1839, the first American daguerreotypes were being made. At that time, there were almost 17 million potential customers here for those artists, daguerreotypists, daguerreans, or daguerreians, as the practitioners of this magical art chose to call themselves, who wanted to make immortality available to the masses. Except not all of these people could enjoy this new opportunity. Almost 2 ½ million, about 15% of the total American population, were owned as slaves. The 1840 census recorded only 377,757 African Americans out of the entire population who were free to visit the studio of the daguerreotypist of their choice to have a "likeness" taken if they could afford it.

The daguerreotype process essentially creates a colorless photographic image upon a silver coated copper plate. Before being exposed to chemicals that made the plate light sensitive, the daguerreotypist buffed the silver on one side until it was highly reflective like a mirror. This accounts for the unique characteristic of this format which requires the plate to be held or observed at an angle that minimizes the reflection in order to view image on its surface. No other photographic format has this unique appearance.   And like your reflection in a mirror, the image on the silver plate is usually reversed. Any words seen on books or signs will probably be reversed unless the maker used a camera that was equipped to "laterally correct" this effect. Since there is no intermediate negative made in the process, each silver plate is an unique original and a true one of a kind. If a person wanted to have more than one daguerreotype of themselves, the artist had to prepare and expose another plate while the subject sat in front of the camera or the process could be used to copy an existing daguerreotype. This copying would also result in correcting any reversal effect in the original. The daguerreotypist often added color to the cheeks of the subject using powders and a fine brush. For an additional fee, the entire image could be hand tinted and, if the artist was skillful, a realistic color image would result.

The sizes of the plates became standardized during the era with the following being the most commonly used:

Full–plate: 6 ½ x 8 ½ inches
Half-plate: 4 ¼ x 5 ½ inches
Quarter-plate: 3 ¼ x 4 ¼ inches
Sixth-plate: 2 ¾ x 3 ¼ inches
Ninth-plate: 2 x 2 ½ inches
Sixteenth-plate: 1 ⅜ x 1 ⅝ inches

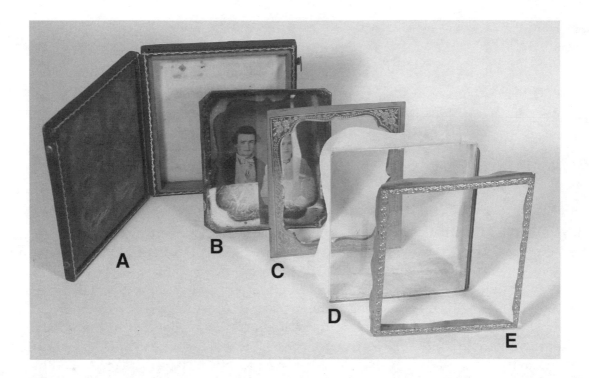

The components of a daguerreotype include the miniature case (A), the daguerreotype plate (B), the mat (C), the cover glass and paper tape seal (D), and the preserver (E) which is usually found added to images made in 1847 or later.

Because of their fragile nature and reverence people had for these daguerreotypes, the plate first had a brass mat placed on it followed by a piece of cover glass. Paper tape was then applied to seal the edges of this sandwich together. By 1847, a thin brass rim called a preserver was added which framed the daguerreotype package and its presence helps to date daguerreotypes to this or a later period. Then the daguerreotype package of the plate, mat, cover glass and possibly a preserver was then usually placed in a "miniature case."

Before the invention of the daguerreotype, people wanting small likenesses of loved ones paid skilled artists to paint their portraits on thin sheets of ivory or paper. These painted "miniatures" were housed in embossed leather or paper covered wooden "miniature cases" which were readily adapted to hold daguerreotypes. Thermoplastic or Union cases, sometimes incorrectly referred to as being made from "gutta percha" (named after the resin from the gutta-percha tree which was not used to make cases), were molded from a plastic composite to house them as well. Many designs were created to decorate these cases which have also made them collectable. (See "Additional Resources" for books that will help in determining their rarity and value.)

Daguerreotypists employed several methods to sign their work. Some stamped their names on the mat covering the image. Studio names and locations could be included on the velvet pad inside the miniature case opposite the image. Printed cards were sometimes placed on the back of the plate under the preserver or pasted inside the case compartment behind the image. Daguerreotypists also wrote their names inside the cases behind the image. A few daguerreans even scratched their names on the silver plate. The addition of a daguerreotypist's name provides another important clue for dating the image. Much work has been done over the years by dedicated researchers seeking to identify where and

Daguerreotypes of slaves are rare and in great demand. The sixth-plate daguerreotype of the unidentified nurse with her young charge (left) is the type that is most frequently found. The half-plate of the house boy with the master's daughter (right) is very rare in size and subject matter and could command a price well into five figures among collectors.

when these early photographers operated. Checking their published directories (see "Additional Resources") can often limit the date for the studio sitting to a narrow window of time.

The earliest daguerreotypes cost as much as five dollars — a week's wages for many, making the medium available to only the well heeled of the day. But over time prices dropped which soon placed the medium within the reach of most who sought immortality on a shiny silver plate. Former slave Frederick Douglass, himself no stranger to the daguerrean studio, noted that as a result of "the wonderful discovery and invention" by Daguerre, "Men of all conditions may see themselves as others see them. What was once the exclusive luxury of the rich and great is now within the reach of all...The smallest town now has a Daguerrian [sic] Gallery."

Some of the operators (another term used to describe the person behind the camera) were African Americans, and a few were able to establish their own galleries around the country. James P. Ball and partner Alexander Thomas, the Goodridge Brothers (Glenalvin, Wallace and William), James Lyon, and Augustus Washington are known to have operated their own studios. Others, including black women, may yet be found to have worked with this new medium. The subjects for their lenses, however, remained predominantly white.

Care and Preservation

Ninth-plate daguerreotype of an unidentified free black girl taken in New York City by Thomas Walsh who gilded her jewelry. The discoloration around the edges of the mat is due to tarnishing of the silver plate. This can be corrected, but it should only be undertaken by a conservator.

Though the stability of the copper plate of the daguerreotype seems to indicate otherwise, the daguerreotype is extremely fragile and any action taken to preserve it should only be done by a very experienced collector or professional conservator. One of the problems that may affect the plate over the years is tarnish — a blue haze or discoloration that forms on anything silver. NEVER touch or attempt to otherwise clean a daguerreotype. Common tarnish removers found in stores can cause irreversible damage to the plate and image. The surface of the daguerreotype is also so fragile that the slightest touch can produce scratches or wipes that are permanent. Another problem is the decomposition of the cover glass. This glass may appear cloudy and seemingly have drops of moisture underneath. Nineteenth century glass is much less stable than that made today and the presence of these problems indicates deterioration of the glass which, if left unchecked, can harm the surface of the daguerreotype if it has not already done so. Replacement of the glass and the resealing of the image with "acid free" archival quality tape should again only be undertaken by an expert! To locate proper help, contact the curator of photography at a state historical society or large museum for recommendations. (Conservationists specializing in photography are also listed in "Additional Resources.")

Collecting Tips

Outdoor daguerreotypes are uncommon and those with African Americans are very rare. This is a close-up of a sixth-plate daguerreotype taken of the furniture business of James Frost that includes several black men posed around the entrance. This is either a copy of a daguerreotype or the camera had a special device to correct the image since the sign is not laterally reversed.

Daguerreotypes have received a lot of interest in recent years and have been the subject of museum exhibits, books, and media attention after long being ignored except by a small number of dedicated collectors. Consequently, the prices commanded for these silver plates have continually risen, especially for those with images of African Americans. In light of the relatively small free black population during the daguerrean era, ALL daguerreotypes that picture them should be considered rare and valuable. The following tips should also help to identify those with the greatest value:

— Condition may not be as critical in evaluating the value of a daguerreotype or any photograph featuring African Americans. While those in excellent condition are important, those with problems should not be discounted as they would be if the subjects were not black. A large portion of surviving images of African American have condition problems which often speaks to the life experience of many black people and the low regard others have had for their photographs until recently.

— Daguerreotypes signed by any of the African American daguerreans are desirable and artistically superior examples of their work bring an added premium. African American subjects recorded by black daguerreans are especially prized.

— Daguerreotypes of famous black Americans are extremely valuable. Identified portraits of any blacks will add a premium to their value since the names of most subjects in daguerreotypes, black or white, have been lost in time.

— As with precious gems, bigger is better and daguerreotypes of African Americans that are a quarter-plate size or larger will command prices comparable to their size. The sixth-plate was the most common size made during the era and it along with the cheaper ninth-plate are the most commonly encountered with black subjects.

— Daguerreotypes of black subjects with the tools of their trade, usually referred to as occupational daguerreotypes, are very rare and valuable. Black musicians, firemen, and soldiers are also very rare and important.

— The most common daguerreotype of African Americans is that of a valued house slave posed with the owner's family. The female nurse posed with children was the most frequently taken. Daguerreotypes of a "house boy" with his white charges are much rarer. Family portraits that included a favored slave are uncommon and very desirable among collectors as well. Portraits of slaves by themselves are also very rare and important. Few ever had the money or opportunity to sit for a daguerreotype so they would have had to been a particular favorite of a master to receive such treatment.

— Daguerreotypes of groups of African Americans are uncommon. Portraits of black mothers with their own children are also uncommon and those of black families, especially with the father present, are extremely rare.

— Outdoor daguerreotypes are uncommon and any that include black subjects are very rare. Outdoor daguerreotypes by black daguerreotypists are also very rare and have commanded record prices at auction.

— Some collectors place a premium on daguerreotypes that have never been "restored." However, replacement of the original cover glass and professional cleaning using approved archival methods are acceptable to many. It may be useful to preserve remnants of the paper seal since it could provide clues for future attribution of unsigned examples. Photograph the artifact before undertaking any conservation procedures.

— Rising prices for images coupled with modern technology opens the door to the creation of fake "vintage" photographs in any format. Because of the high level of difficulty in making a daguerreotype, the use of the process to make fakes is not generally a problem. But there are people that have become proficient in making daguerreotypes and fakes do exist. If you are purchasing an expensive photograph in any format, you may want to get a written guarantee of its age from the seller.

Focal Point: A Visit J.P. Ball's Gallery

The grand reception room in "Ball's Great Daguerrian Gallery of the West."

On a bright spring day in 1854, Rebecca Hercules traveled by carriage to Cincinnati for a very important day in her life and that of her three children. For the first time, they were all going to visit a daguerreotype studio to have their group portrait taken. Living on a farm in the Ohio countryside, they had to travel to the city for the opportunity to be recorded for posterity.   Mrs. Hercules' husband James was unable to make the trip since he had to tend to the farm while his family was away. But the modest success of his place made it possible for his wife to make him the special gift of a daguerreotype of Rebecca and their three children, Eliza Jane, Barbra and Christopher. Reading the advertisement for galleries in the local newspapers, Mrs. Hercules had decided to visit the gallery of the African American daguerrean James P. Ball. His studio was noted for possessing "the best materials and the finest instruments" and that the daguerreotypes made there were taken "with an accuracy and softness of expression unsurpassed by any establishment in the Union."

James P. Ball was born free in Virginia in 1825. While visiting the resort spa at White Sulphur Springs, Virginia, he made the acquaintance of John B. Bailey, a daguerreotypist from Boston. Bailey revealed to Ball the mysteries of this new daguerrean process which inspired him to decide to take up the practice of daguerreotypy as well. Later that year, he opened a daguerrean studio in Cincinnati though it closed in just three months due to a lack of customers. From there he traveled as an itinerant artist setting up his studio for a time in Pittsburgh and then in Virginia. After working as a waiter in a Richmond hotel to raise sufficient capital, he opened his studio in that city in 1846 that enjoyed some success. The following year, he returned back to Ohio working again as an itinerant daguerrean and in 1849, he opened a studio in Cincinnati and hired his brother Thomas Ball to work in the establishment. This venture soon became one of the largest and most lavish in the Midwest.

As business grew, Ball relocated in 1851 to 28 West 4th Street where he and his brother opened "Ball's Great Daguerrian Gallery of the West." Located on the most fashionable thoroughfare in Cincinnati, this new gallery occupied the three upper floors of the large building. The gilt letters on the black painted signs by the street entrance beckoned patrons to enter and experience the wonders of the Ball studio. After leaving her carriage at the stable, Rebecca walked with her children up the steps and into what must have seemed to be another world to a farmer's family. The expansive 20 by 40 foot room was unlike anything like they had ever seen before. At one end was a counter, where they were greeted perhaps by Mr. Ball or one of his employees. After placing her name in the gallery register, the assistant displayed the different sizes of daguerreotypes offered by the gallery along with the various styles of cases and frames available to house the silver plate. He explained how, for an extra fee, the plate could be tinted by his skilled colorist making it a remarkable masterpiece of art. For her special sitting, Rebecca chose to have an expensive half-plate daguerreotype portrait made of her family. The plate was to be tinted by the colorist as well and the final package was to be housed in a fine embossed leather case. The mother and her children were then ushered into the main reception gallery.

The fancy papered walls, trimmed in gold leaf and flowers, the lush woven carpet, and two large gilt pier mirrors lured the family to marvel at the room's opulence. Sculpted statues of the goddesses of Poetry, Music, Science, Religion, and Purity lined one long wall. Opposite them were the shiny silver plates of 187 Ball daguerreotypes featuring many portraits of local citizens and famous visitors of the day including singer Jenny Lind, "the Swedish Nightingale." Six paintings by black artist Robert Duncanson, who had also worked for Ball as a colorist, adorned the walls as well. Upholstered chairs of the highest quality were available for patrons to relax upon while waiting to be called for their sitting. Notes from a parlor piano filled the air providing gentle background music as patrons enjoyed the sumptuously appointed gallery.

After a few minutes passed, Mrs. Hercules and children were called for their sitting. They climbed the wooden steps to the top floor of the building where they were ushered into the studio where Daguerre's magic was performed. A glass skylight in the ceiling bathed the large open room with the natural illumination needed to make the daguerreotype. In front of a plain canvas backdrop in the middle of the floor sat an upholstered chair and a small damask covered table. Behind stood the "iron instrument of torture" as it was sometimes called or head-clamp on a stand that stilled the subject during the exposure. Reflectors on either side of the tableau enabled the operator to adjust the lighting for the scene. On a stand several feet away sat the instrument that made the daguerreotype possible — the camera. The imposing instrument was really a light-proof wooden box that had a brass tube on the front that held the lens. A slot at the top allowed the insertion of the daguerreotype plate.

The family was probably greeted by Mr. Ball himself, who would have wanted to be the one to take such an expensive daguerreotype rather than leave it to one of his other operators. The artist ushered Mrs. Hercules to the posing chair where she was instructed to sit while her

Woodcut illustration from an advertisement for a daguerrean studio. As the daguerreotypist looked at his watch to time his exposure, he removed a cap from the lens of the camera to expose the plate. The illumination for the sitting comes from the glass skylight.

three children were positioned around her. While engaged in light conversation, he busied himself with arranging his subjects, setting the clamps of the headstands to the back of their heads to prevent movement, and adjusting the reflectors to achieve the proper balance of light and shade. He then retreated to the rear of the camera to view the scene. While covering his head with a black drape, the operator peered at the ground-glass in the rear of the camera that enabled him to focus the lens and study the composition. Any final changes were then made. Once satisfied, he removed the focusing glass from the camera and placed a cap over the lens. The picture was almost ready to be taken.

The headstand was used in J.P. Ball's studio and other photography galleries throughout most of the 19th century to keep subject's still during exposure times that could last from 5 seconds to as long as 20 seconds.

The daguerreotypist was handed a wooden plate holder by an assistant that had been brought up from the workroom downstairs. Inside was the silver plated copper sheet that had just been treated with several chemicals which made it light sensitive. He carried the light proof container back to the studio, inserted it into the camera, and then slipped open a sliding panel on one side of the carrier. A crucial step now commenced.

True daguerrean artists were guided by the standards of the day that identified a person's expression as one of the key elements of a successful daguerreotype. Mr. Ball continued to engage in conversation with the family until experience told him that he had coaxed just the right "look." At that critical moment, sitters were told to hold their pose as the operator removed the cap from the lens. The plate was exposed in the camera for several seconds (the correct amount being dictated by experience), and then the cap was replaced ending the exposure. As the sitters returned downstairs to the reception room, the daguerreotypist closed the plate-holder to prepare for the next step of the process.

After being carried to a darkened workroom a floor below, the plate was removed from the carrier and was placed in a special developing chamber. Here the vapors of heated mercury caused the image to appear. After a few minutes, the plate was removed and washed in several solutions. The first "fixed" the image or made it insensitive to light, and the second increased its brilliance. Then it was rinsed with water and carefully dried over an alcohol lamp. Once accomplished, Mr. Ball's colorist used a fine brush to touch some pink to the girl's dresses and everyone's cheeks. Lastly, the delicate plate had a thin brass mat and protective piece of glass placed over it. When the edges of the sandwich had been sealed with paper tape, it was enclosed in the brass preserver. The small package was then ready for presentation.

Perhaps about twenty minutes had passed before Ball called the anxious family over to view the results of their ordeal. Upon the polished silver plate framed by the golden mat was the sitters' likenesses forever frozen in time. If the outcome was satisfactory, the package was placed in the "miniature case" selected earlier from Ball's varied stock. After final costs were calculated, the proprietor presented the bill. As was the custom with better galleries, Ball's patrons did not pay for daguerreotypes until completely satisfied. Once Rebecca paid the clerk in cash (credit cards did not yet exist), the Hercules family departed with their prized package in hand. They had now joined the exclusive legion of Americans recorded for posterity by a J.P. Ball daguerreotype.

Mrs. Hercules chose an embossed leather miniature case to house her family's half-plate daguerreotype. The design is typical of those commonly used during the period.

Half-plate daguerreotype made by African American daguerreotypist James P. Ball of Rebecca Hercules and her children Eliza Jane, Christopher, and Barbra reproduced in the actual size of the original. The mat is stamped with Ball's name and "Cincinnati" for the location of his gallery. The daguerreotypist's colorist added a delicate pink tinting to each of the girls' dresses. The excellent preparation and processing of the silver plate along with the successful composition and expression of the family created an outstanding example of Ball's technical and artistic skills as a daguerrean.

Of the 3,950,546 slaves in the United States in 1860, few ever had the opportunity at that time to be recorded by the camera's lens. This anonymous sixth-plate ambrotype of unidentified children included this handwritten label stating "Peculiar Institution." This term was widely used in the South to refer to the "institution" of slavery. Judging by its addition along with the simple, identical dresses of the young girls who are seen holding hands, it is probable that these children were slaves and sisters. Perhaps this ambrotype was paid for by an abolitionist and the note was added to point out the horrors of a system that held innocent children in bondage. Unfortunately, their story has been lost in time.

THE AMBROTYPE

The daguerreotype reigned as the primary photographic process in the United States from 1840 through the mid 1850s. The limitations of its expensive and delicate silver plate with its highly reflective surface, however, spurred a search for an even better way for capturing time. A discovery made in England in 1851 prepared the way for a technique that was most instrumental in recording the face of America for much of the rest of the 19th century. This new method was named the collodion or "wet-plate" process.

In the wet-plate method, glass was used as the base for the photographic chemicals instead of the silver plate of the daguerrean system. A sheet of glass (or even blackened sheet iron) was coated by a syrupy solution called "collodion." This transparent fluid was allowed to dry to a tacky consistency at which time the plate was dipped in a bath of silver nitrate. The resulting coating was light sensitive as long as the chemicals remained tacky or "wet." After exposure in a camera, development with a solution of pyrogallic acid and fixing (making light insensitive) in a bath of thiosulfate, a negative was produced. This collodion process and the glass negative served as the basis for most photography until the emergence of flexible "film" at the end of the 19th century. With its affordable price and the proliferation of photography studios, particularly in the North after the outbreak of the Civil War, most Americans regardless of their race were eventually recorded for posterity by the wet-plate process.

The collodion process was used to produce several types of photographs that are commonly encountered among old family photographs today. The earliest format created from the wet-plate process was called the ambrotype derived from the Greek word *ambrotos* meaning immortal. From about 1855 through the early 1860s, the ambrotype immortalized many faces of the past.

To make an ambrotype, a thin or light negative was produced on the glass plate by some additional chemical treatment to the wet-plate process. When a dark backing was placed behind the plate, the appearance of a positive image was created. (Like the daguerreotype, each plate is unique since it is the actual one exposed in the camera.) This backing could be achieved several ways. Blackened varnish was painted on the back of the plate opposite the emulsion side, a piece of black paper or paper painted with the black varnish could be cut to size and placed behind the image, and sometimes a piece of black fabric was inserted. Dark ruby colored glass could also get the same effect if placed either behind the negative or if it was used as the base for the light sensitive chemicals. All of these can be encountered in ambrotypes, but the black varnish technique is most commonly found. And like the daguerreotype, an embossed brass mat was placed on the plate and an additional piece of cover glass could then be added to protect the image if the emulsion side of the plate is placed face up. This sandwich was then held together by the embossed brass preserver like those used earlier.

To make a wet-plate negative, a photographer (left) coats a sheet of glass with collodion which is then dipped in a bath of silver nitrate. After exposure in a camera, development and processing, a negative is produced. When backed with dark material (right), the negative turns into a positive image.

The standard sizes for ambrotypes (with mat and preserver) were the same as those used with the daguerreotype along with a new eighth-plate "carte de visite" size:

> Full-plate: 6 ½ x 8 ½ inches
> Half-plate: 4 ¼ x 5 ½ inches
> Quarter-plate: 3 ¼ x 4 ¼ inches
> Sixth-plate: 2 ¾ x 3 ¼ inches
> Eighth-plate (carte de visite): 2 ¼ x 3 ½ inches
> Ninth-plate: 2 x 2 ½ inches
> Sixteenth-plate: 1 ⅜ x 1 ⅝ inches

The sixth-plate was again the most commonly made size. Miniature cases covered in embossed paper or leather, or those composition union cases that had been used for daguerreotypes, were now used to house ambrotypes as well.

As with the daguerreotype, photographers employed several methods to sign their work. Some stamped their names on the mat surrounding the image. Studio names and locations could be included on the velvet pad inside the miniature case opposite the image. Printed cards were sometimes placed behind the image under the preserver or pasted inside the case compartment behind the image. Sometimes photographers wrote their names inside the cases behind the image. A few photographers, such as Charles Rees of Virginia, actually scratched their name into the emulsion of the image.

Subjects of these images are sometimes identified as well. Identifications can be found on slips of paper attached to the case padding or placed behind the image in the case. Sometimes names are written on the case behind the image. Caution must be taken when using these identities, however, since images were easy to exchange between cases of the same size. Names of sitters have also been found written on the edge of the preserver folded behind the image!

A nurse posed with her charge (left) for this half-plate ambrotype. Though she was probably a slave, her dress and her appearance in this more expensive size image indicates that she was a valued member of the family. The mother in the quarter-plate on the right was able to pose with her own child dressed in the latest fashion. African American women during this time were less likely to be recorded with their own children.

Because of the need for a nearby darkroom to prepare and develop the plate while light sensitive chemicals were still tacky, the vast majority of ambrotypes were taken inside studios. In towns or cities, studios were usually located on the top floor of a building situated so it could best catch the northern light that was most desirable for photography. Those who made ambrotypes in the field usually operated inside a specially designed tent or wagon that had a skylight opening built in the roof. Subjects (individuals, pairs, or small groups) were posed seated or standing directly facing the camera or in three-quarter pose depending on the artistic skill of the photographer. Props may have included chairs and tables for subjects to stand or sit next to. Books were commonly added to suggest the subject's literacy though titles and any other writing may appear backwards since ambrotypes, like daguerreotypes, were often laterally reversed. Some studios included columns and drapes to enhance the composition as well. Backdrops range from plain to painted scenes with classical, naturalistic or military themes after the start of the Civil War. Soldiers often posed with accouterments and weapons, both personal and those provided by the photographer, to enhance their militaristic impression. Civilians sometimes posed holding tools or other objects that symbolized their occupations.

By working near a fixed studio, darkroom wagon or portable field outfit, photographers sometimes made outdoor ambrotypes, but these are far less common than indoor images. Ambrotypes were usually made for a specific customer and the use of the unique glass plate as the basis for the image limited large-scale duplication.

Care and Preservation

Sixth-plate ambrotype of an unidentified member of the Bishop family in Baltimore. Over the years, the mat, cover glass and preserver had been removed and had to be replaced. Fortunately, the emulsion on the glass plate had not been damaged. Though this surface is not quite as fragile as that of the daguerreotype, it can be easily scratched and abraded if exposed.

Since glass was used as the base for the light sensitive emulsion, the ambrotype plate does not suffer from the tarnishing experienced by the daguerreotype. The process, however, does have its own preservation problems. Perhaps the greatest is the fragility of the glass plate which can crack or shatter if dropped or otherwise mishandled. Care should always be taken in handling an image within or removed from its miniature case. The emulsion on the glass plate should NEVER be touched since this can produce a scratch or wipe. NEVER let any liquid come in contact with the plate since the emulsion may dissolve. One of the biggest problems with ambrotypes is the deterioration of the black varnish backing that may have cracked or flaked off over time. Placing a piece of black paper inside the case behind the image can sometimes be a satisfactory temporary solution. The cover glass may have also become hazy from deterioration. It can be carefully lifted off and cleaned after removing the preserver, but be careful not to touch the image surface. You may prefer, however, to have a skilled conservationist undertake this or any other restoration. Contact the curator of photography at your state historical society for recommendations.

Collecting Tips

Quarter-plate ambrotype of an anonymous couple posed with their well dressed servant. Portraits such as this are very desirable among collectors. As with daguerreotypes, the image in an ambrotype is often laterally reversed so this gentleman actually posed with his right hand in his vest. Courtesy of Howard R. McManus

As with the daguerreotype, ambrotypes of African Americans are scarce and important. The free black population of the United States numbered approximately 477,000 in 1860, just 1 ½ % of the country's total population! Few of this number were photographed and fewer still have had their ambrotype portraits survive. Most of the "Collecting Tips" for the daguerreotype apply to the ambrotype as well. A few are worth re-emphasizing:

— African American photographs in all formats very often have condition problems. The scarcity and importance of the subject matter should far outweigh any physical problems the image has suffered. The power of digital restoration can save many otherwise "lost" and damaged images.

— Portraits of nurses with their charges are eagerly sought by collectors. Servants posed with their owners or with owners and their families are also very desirable. Images of slaves by themselves are very rare and only a special relationship with their owner would have resulted in an individual portrait. Additional evidence should exist, however, to support the conclusion that the subject was truly a slave at the time of their sitting.

During the 19th century, people were proud of their work, no matter how humble, and they sometimes posed for their photographs with tools and other objects that indicated their job. These are known as "occupational" portraits among collectors. In this anonymous ninth-plate ambrotype, this young boy posed wearing his apron and holding the pottery bowl of a tobacco pipe. (Tobacco could be smoked after a hollow stem was inserted in a hole on the side.) All of this indicates that he was probably employed in a pottery factory, though we do not know if he was a slave or free. Occupational portraits of African Americans from this era are uncommon and those that document factory related child labor are extremely rare.

It cannot be assumed that African Americans in daguerreotypes or ambrotypes are always slaves. There needs to be additional evidence to support this conclusion. These anonymous ambrotypes were found in Maryland which had both slaves and the largest free black population in the United States in 1860.

— Bigger is also better. Ambrotypes of African Americans in quarter plate sizes or larger were more expensive and exist in fewer numbers. Subsequently, full-plate portraits are extremely rare.

— Ambrotypes by black photographers, especially of black subjects, are also very desirable.

— Because of the need for a nearby darkroom to prepare and develop the wet-plate, outdoor ambrotypes are scarce. Those with black subjects are even rarer and very important as well.

— Portraits in which black subjects pose with the tools of their trade along with images of soldiers, firemen, and musicians are rare and important.

— Among photography collectors, daguerreotypes are most highly prized and usually command higher prices than other cased images like the ambrotype. But the scarcity of African American ambrotypes along with unusual subject manner can also cause them to become comparably priced.

— The wet-plate process has been revived by a number of people which gives rise to a concern over fakes. Ambrotypes of modern re-enactors, both military and civilian, exist and can be convincing enough to be passed off as actual 19th century images. The process has also been used to copy vintage photographs. Caution should be exercised when buying any expensive image. Get a written guarantee of authenticity from the dealer with any major purchase.

Focal Point: Mr. Goodridge's Cat

Sixth-plate ambrotype by Glenalvin Goodridge, ca. 1860.

Among the few documented African American photographers working in the United States before the Civil War was Glenalvin Goodridge in York, Pennsylvania. Glenalvin's father, William, had been born a slave in Maryland. When his mother was sold to a Baltimore doctor, William was apprenticed to a York minister and tanner who eventually gave the young Goodridge his freedom. William then went on to achieve some success as a local barber, real estate speculator and railroad freight shipper.

William's oldest son, Glenalvin, was born in 1829 and, by 1848, he was a teacher in a private school in York and it was noted that he maintained a daguerreotype gallery at his father's home that he operated "during leisure hours." It is believed that Glenalvin learned daguerreotypy from Joseph Reinhart, an itinerant daguerreotypist that had visited York from April through June, 1847. Soon after Reinhart's departure, Glenalvin announced the opening of a "Goodridge's Daguerrean Rooms."   While he continued his teaching, Goodridge operated his daguerrean studio on the side since it was still difficult to make a living with a full time gallery in the local community. By 1850, the studio was relocated to a building owned by his father on the town square and Glenalvin joined the ranks of professional daguerreans. In just a few years, his daguerreotypes began to get national recognition and receive awards at local fairs.

The year 1855 marked a major change in Goodridge's business when he introduced the "ambrotype" to the York community. The new format was made from the wet-plate collodion process that used glass instead of a silver plate as the base for the light sensitive chemicals. Cheaper to make, the format was also regarded as an improvement over the daguerreotype since it did not have the "peculiar glare" that required the plate to be viewed at a particular angle to be seen. Goodridge obtained a license for James Cutting's patent system that sealed the image side of the glass negative to a cover glass using balsam of fir as the sealant . Consequently, some Goodridge ambrotypes are found that have "Patent July 4th and 11th, 1854" stamped on the brass mat along with Glenalvin's name. This marked the high point of Glenalvin's photographic endeavor.

Goodridge's studio enjoyed success among the citizen's of York despite his being a man of color. Most existing examples of his work are sixth-plate portraits of individuals, couples, mothers with their children, and post mortems (deceased people). Outdoor views are rare but do exist. Among the most unusual is the that of a lone cat posed on the caned seat of a simple chair in his studio. Since the days of the daguerreotype, people used the new medium to record those subjects that were most important to them. Consequently, they brought along their dogs, cats, and even birds to pose for the camera's eye. Cats were a particular challenge for the photographer with exposure times that lasted several seconds and are much rarer subjects in early photographs. Taking them into an unfamiliar place where they were surrounded with strange smells, odd equipment, backdrops and bright skylights made many a feline even more skittish. When they do appear, they are often held tightly by their owner to prevent movement (no headstands existed for pets). Cats posed by themselves are very rare.

This sixth-plate portrait may well record a valued member of the Goodridge family. Perhaps Glenalvin patiently waited for his pet to jump up into his posing chair and lay down for his sitting. The warmth of the light made this a cozy setting surrounded with objects and people with which the pet had already grown familiar. Once on the chair, Glenalvin had to focus his camera and prepare the glass for his wet-plate negative in a nearby darkroom and rush it to the camera for exposing. Since the plate was only light sensitive for a few minutes while still tacky, it could not be prepared ahead of time. Once placed into the camera, a slide was removed from one side of the wooden plate holder and everything was now ready. The photographer probably made a noise or called his pet's name to get the cat to look at the camera. At that critical moment, Goodridge uncapped the lens for several seconds. Then the cap was placed back on the lens ending the exposure. Once in the darkroom, the glass plate was removed from the plate holder and processed revealing a thin negative of his furry subject. It was then backed with black varnish to make the familiar positive image. Like the daguerreotype, this had a mat and sheet of glass placed over it along with the preserver to hold the package together. This sandwich was then inserted into the embossed leather case that bore the imprint of Goodridge's Gallery on the opposite velvet pad. Though the cat had moved his head just slightly, the resulting portrait was a technical success and rare achievement among daguerreotypes and ambrotypes.

Despite competition from other studios that cropped up in York, Goodridge's gallery continued to operate until 1859. During that year, Glenalvin abandoned his photography business for a time and returned to teaching. This was possibly a result of the financial failure of his father's business in whose building his gallery operated. He reopened "Goodridge's American Photographic Gallery" in 1861 with his brother William as partner and was successful enough to open another studio in neighboring Columbia. Unfortunately, this venture ultimately failed and Glenalvin died in 1867 from tuberculosis. His brothers and family went on to run a successful photography business in Saginaw, Michigan, that lasted into the 1920s.

*Anonymous quarter-plate melainotype of an unidentified child.   We can only speculate why the photographer
of an upscale studio made this compelling portrait of the young school boy.   If the child's family had been
wealthy enough to have his likeness taken, they probably would have not had him pose in his patched trousers.*

3

THE TINTYPE (MELAINOTYPE)

In the mid-1850s, a unique format was developed in the United States based on the collodion wet-plate process that survived well into the early 20th century and it was particularly popular among African Americans judging by the relatively large number of surviving examples today. Known technically as the ferrotype (from *ferro* for iron) or melainotype (from *melaino* for black or dark), it became commonly referred to as the tintype though tin was never used in the process. In this form of photography, blackened sheet iron was coated with the collodion/silver nitrate mixture that rendered the plate light sensitive as long as the chemicals remained tacky. Once exposed in a camera and developed, an image appeared on the plate that was fixed and coated with varnish. Like the ambrotype, there was no intermediate negative — the metal base is the plate placed in the camera so each tintype is unique (unless the photographer used a multi-lens camera that made several exposures on a plate at one sitting which was then cut apart after processing). Photographers often applied red tinting to the subjects cheeks and gold to buttons, watch chains, and jewelry. Some large tintypes are encountered that are completely hand colored which, if done skillfully, creates a remarkable image of reality. The result was portrait that was durable and cheap and was especially popular for portraits of soldiers during the Civil War. Photographer David Bachrach, Jr. noted in his memoirs that "the making of tintypes of the soldiers for a dollar each was a very profitable business" since each tintype cost only ten cents to make. Photographers often followed the Union armies offering to photographically immortalize soldiers, including African Americans in 1863 when they too could enlist.

The standard sizes of the tintype approximate that of the daguerreotype and ambrotype since miniature cases had been designed for the earlier formats. However, the "gem" size was a new addition.

Full-plate: 6 ½ x 8 ½ inches
Half-plate: 4 ¼ x 5 ½ inches
Quarter-plate: 3 ¼ x 4 ¼ inches
Sixth-plate: 2 ¾ x 3 ¼ inches
Carte de Visite Size: 2 ¼ x 3 ½ inches
Ninth-plate: 2 x 2 ½ inches
Sixteenth-plate: 1 ⅜ x 1 ⅝ inches
Gem: ¾ x 1 inch (usually mounted within or attached
        to carte de visite size paper card). Special "gem"
        albums with specially designed pages were also
        created to hold these small tintypes.

This early melainotype plate is marked with the Neff's Patent stamp and is an indicator of an early example of a tintype dating from the late 1850s to the early 1860s. William and his son Peter Neff bought the patent rights for the melainotype from the inventor Hamilton Smith in 1856.

Earlier ferrotype plates were sometimes stamped by rival plate manufacturers "Melainotype/ Neff's Pat. 19Feb56" or variants of "Griswold's Patented Oct. 21 1856" (very uncommon). These are found on plates from the late 1850s through the early 1860s and are a good indicator of an image made within that time frame. Early plates were usually covered with a mat and cover glass along with the preserver that held the sandwich together. It was then placed in a miniature case. Their appearance in the case can sometimes look very much like an ambrotype and the difference can only be determined by gently removing the image package from the case and looking at the back to see if the plate is metal. This does not always resolve the difference because blackened metal plates were sometimes used to back ambrotypes. Then it may be necessary to remove the preserver to determine the composition of the plate bearing the image. Seek the help of a professional if you are inexperienced with taking a case image apart.

Additional information may be present to help date a tintype. Photographers sometimes attached paper labels to the back of plates (which rarely survive), placed trade cards behind the image or in the miniature case, wrote their names into the miniature case behind the image, stamped their names on the mat, or had an embossed velvet pad inside the miniature case opposite the image. Ferrotypes mounted in paper sleeves often have the name of the photographer printed on the back or sometimes on the bottom of the front. Published directories of photographers (see "Additional Resources") may help to determine a time frame for the photographer's business and when your tintype was made. Like paper photographs, tintypes were also subject to taxation during the Civil War. Federal revenue stamps were pasted to the back of plates (or placed behind the image inside the miniature case) after the imposition of stamp duties from August 1, 1864 until August 1, 1866. Photographers were supposed to cancel the stamps with their initials and date; unfortunately for historians, many did not completely follow this requirement.

Identities of subjects can be found written on the paper mounts, inside cases, or even scratched into the photographic emulsion or on the back of the plate. During the Civil War, many ferrotypes of soldiers were sold with only a brass mat placed over them with the four corners bent behind to attach it. No cover glass, preserver, or miniature case was used to protect and house the image. Evidence also indicates that some soldiers purchased ferrotypes that were not mounted on or placed in paper sleeves or housed in cases at all. These plates were then particularly susceptible to damage over time.

Care and Preservation

The tintypes of this unidentified couple that are still housed in their original paper sleeves. Their stylish dress indicates that they date from the 1870s. The unknown photographer highlighted the gentleman's watch chain in gold and tinted both of their ties in blue. Over four and a half million African Americans were now free to visit the photographer's studio during this time.

Because of the use of sheet iron as the base for the tintype, the image is seemingly a strong and stable photographic medium. However, care must be taken when handling and storing them since they are really a delicate format. Plates can be bent and creased which can cause permanent damage to the thin layer of emulsion bearing the image on its surface. The emulsion can also be scratched and otherwise abraded if left unprotected. Exposure to extremes in temperature can cause the emulsion to fracture and craze much like the surface of an old painting. Moisture and high humidity can cause the plate to rust and make the emulsion's coating stick to any surface that lays on top of it. Rust can also cause the emulsion to flake off of the plate. Transparent archival sleeves (made from polypropylene or polyester) can be purchased to protect the exposed surface of uncased plates (see "Additional Resources"). No attempt should be taken to "restore" an original plate except by a professional photograph conservator. The plate can be copied to create a digital file that can be enhanced, often with remarkable success. These copies can then be enlarged, framed and distributed to family members while the original plates are carefully stored in acid free boxes in a safe place with controlled constant temperatures and low humidity (no attics or basements).

Collecting Tips

Portraits of "Buffalo Soldiers" who were assigned to western army posts are very collectible. The soldier (left) in this unidentified sixth-plate wears the five button blouse adopted by the army in 1883 and a privately purchased fur hat for protection from the cold on the Great Plains. (Tintypes are usually laterally reversed and his coat buttons appear to be on the left side of his jacket though they were actually on the right.) Studio occupational portraits of African Americans are uncommon in any early photographic format and those, such as this sixth-plate of a group of telephone installers (right), are extremely rare.

Since tintypes were made from the mid 1850s into the early 20th century, they are among the most common early photographs to be found. However, those that bear the images of African Americans remain less common than other segments of the population and are also desirable among collectors. The following guidelines can help determine their collectable value.

— As with the other photographic formats, tintypes of African Americans often have condition problems. Consequently, visually and/or historically interesting images in good or better condition will have increased value as well.

— Size continues to matter since larger plates were more expensive and are less common today. Plates that have been tastefully colored can have their value enhanced as well. This was often done to full-plate tintypes.

— Melainotypes of nurses with their charges are desirable, but usually do not command the prices paid for similar daguerreotypes and ambrotypes. Any tintype of a slave by themselves would be in demand and may sell for a value close to that of an ambrotype or daguerreotype. There will need to be other evidence besides patched or worn clothing to support the conclusion that the subject was truly a slave. There were 476,748 free blacks recorded in the 1860 census.

Tintypes by African American photographers, such as this quarter-plate (left) taken around 1860 by James Presley Ball and Alexander Thomas are very collectible. The style of photograph and the dress of the man (right) posed with his young servant indicates that this was taken after the Civil War and the abolition of slavery.

— Tintypes of black soldiers from the Civil War or the post-war "buffalo soldiers" out west are especially in demand. A total of 178,975 African Americans served in the Union Army and 9,596 in the U.S. Navy during the Civil War. Armed soldiers are always most desirable. Tintypes of soldiers posed with their wives and children are scarce.

— Outdoor tintypes are less common than studio portraits and those that include African Americans are scarce and can command high prices.

— Earlier melainotypes of African Americans that are housed in miniature cases date from the mid-1850s until the early 1860s and are rarer that those from the post Civil War era. Tintypes made after the Civil War are sometimes found housed in miniature cases though this was a less common practice. Plates may have been placed in these cases by the family, but it also may have been done by someone trying to enhance the value of a later tintype by making it appear to have been made earlier. The dress of the subjects and the props used by the photographer along with plate sizes and shape will also offer clues for dating.

— Portraits recording occupations, musicians, pets, and cameras are uncommon and desirable. Post-mortems (studio portraits of someone deceased) of African Americans are rare.

— Numerous individuals are again taking tintypes and the problem with fakes or misrepresented images occurs. It is possible that vintage images could be copied as tintypes and sold as originals. Modern tintypes of either military of civilian living history specialists could fool an untrained eye as well. Purchase high priced tintypes from reputable dealers who provide a written receipt that guarantees the age and authenticity.

This is a carte de visite of the Virginia field studio for Massachusetts photographers' Hall and Judkins. Many enterprising photographers set up temporary studios near the winter camps of the Union army during the Civil War to offer tintypes for one dollar to the thousands of soldiers nearby, including black troops beginning in 1863.

Most portraits of Civil War soldiers were taken in the photographers studio which may have been in a building, a temporary wooden hut, or even a portable tent. Natural light from the skylight above the photographer provided the illumination as the headstand steadied the soldier when the plate was exposed in the camera.

Focal Point: Civil War Soldier Tintypes

Sixth-plate tintype of an unidentified private in the U.S. Colored Troops. A mat with a patriotic theme, a style introduced during the Civil War, was used to cover the plate. The ring around the mat opening is caused by changes over time in the emulsion and cannot be corrected.

    Many of the African American soldiers who served in the Union army during the Civil War were recorded by the tintype process. This was a very popular format offered by photographers that set up near where Union armies camped. Because of the need for a nearby darkroom for plate preparation and development, most portraits were taken inside a studio. This "gallery" may have been in a fixed location in a town or city, or it may have been a simple log hut or tent in the field. Illumination was provided by a roof skylight (even in tents) and settings were usually sparse with a simple table and/or chair prop and a plain or painted (often with an imitation outdoor military camp theme) canvas backdrop. Subjects usually posed standing or seated and were recorded directly facing the camera or in three-quarter pose. Soldiers sometimes included their personal weapons (or props provided by the photographer) to enhance their warrior impression. On occasion, some soldiers were recorded in less conventional poses that interpreted aspects of camp life such as card playing, drinking, and eating. Among collectors, images that differ in pose and/or prop from those most frequently encountered are particularly desirable, but all portraits of black soldiers, especially if they are armed, are valuable and highly sought after by collectors.

    Unlike paper photographs, tintype images taken outside the confines of the studio are less common. Since these images were usually made for a specific customer in a format that produced a one of a kind portrait, mass duplication of images was impractical. Typical outdoor scenes include mounted cavalrymen, groups of soldiers (enlisted and officers), mess groups, individual camps or winter huts, and artillery batteries. Because of their rarity, outdoor tintypes command a premium among collectors depending on their subject matter and condition.

Carte de visite by Josiah Marken taken at Frederick, Maryland, in the early 1860s that has his imprint on the back. A pencil notation identifies this as "Jack Brunner, slave boy owned by Uncle Val." Jack must have been highly regarded slave to have been photographed by himself. Despite the condition, this is a rare and desirable photograph among collectors.

The Carte de Visite

On the eve of the outbreak of the Civil War in 1860, the African American population numbered over 4.4 million out of a total population of about 31 million people in the United States. Only 476,748 blacks were identified as being free in the national census which recorded almost 4 million slaves. Only the most fortunate African Americans initially found themselves recorded through a newly emerging use for the wet-plate process — making paper photographs from glass negatives. The fine detail that could be reproduced coupled with the potential of unlimited duplication caused this process to eventually eclipse almost all other formats from the time of its appearance until the development of dry-plate glass negatives in the early 1880s. By that time, many former slaves and ancestors of slaves began to finally achieve their immortality through photography that had long been available to others.

In this format, the albumen print, recognizable by its purplish sepia tones, was the most commonly produced photograph. These prints were made by first coating a sheet of thin paper with a solution made from potassium iodide and the white of a chicken egg. This sheet was immersed in a bath of silver nitrate to become light sensitive and was kept in darkness until used for printing. To make a photograph, a glass plate negatives was laid directly on the paper that was exposed to sunlight until the desirable print quality was reached. The resulting print was then fixed, washed and dried, and was ready for mounting. The paper print was then trimmed and pasted to cardboard that provided a firm backing for the thin paper. For extra money, the prints could also be hand colored.

The question then was in what size should these paper photographs be made. In Victorian times, it was the practice to leave a calling card when visiting the home of family or a friend. Baskets were often kept in a home's hallway entrance to receive printed or hand signed calling cards. A French photographer is credited with having the idea of gluing a paper photograph onto cardboard about the size of these calling cards. This new format, named the carte de visite (French for "visiting card"), quickly caught on and "cartemania" soon raged in the United States.

Cartes de visite were usually made from glass plate negatives exposed in a special camera with four lenses that produced multiple negatives on a single plate. The plate made several prints on one sheet which were cut out and applied individually to the cardboard backing. Customers usually purchased them by the dozen at a cost of about $5.00. In 1860, photographic albums were introduced that allowed the insertion of cartes into page pockets. This helped to standardize the size of the photographs produced in this format to about 2 ½ x 4 inches (some early cards are a bit larger). The format was used for both studio portrait and outdoor views. Larger prints could be made too, but this required a camera that could hold the bigger glass plates. Enlargements were sometimes made from a "solar camera" that printed through smaller negatives onto larger photographic paper. However, the best results for photographic prints were obtained from placing the light sensitive paper directly under the glass negative and exposing it to daylight.

This carte de visite was taken of a Maryland lady accompanied by her black servant while on a visit to Boston. The card bears the imprint for James W. Black's Boston photograph gallery on the reverse. The federal tax stamp was also included as required beginning August 1, 1864. This example was properly cancelled by Black who used a stamp that included his name and the date December 6, 1864 providing invaluable information for interpreting photographs. Unfortunately, few photographers complied with adding the specific date of cancellation though use of the stamps was widespread. Since slavery was abolished in Maryland under a new state constitution effective November 1, 1864, the servant was a free woman and no longer a slave at the time this photograph was made though slavery was still legal in other states.

The cardboard mounts of the carte de visite encouraged several practices that help in dating these photographs. Photographers usually printed their names and studio addresses on the back of card mounts or attached a label. A few used more elaborate designs and type faces along with engravings of pictures which became more common after the Civil War. Some included their names printed or blind stamped on the front below the print along with a copyright notice if the image was for sale to the general public. A few were marked with just a simple manuscript identification of the photographer. Regardless of how they were signed, a carte de visite may often be dated to a narrow period of time by checking the published directories of photographers (see "Additional Resources"). These directories have biographical information on many (but not all) American photographers that usually include the dates for both a photographer's period of operation and specific studio locations. An additional resource for dating photographs is the presence of revenue stamps affixed to the back of the image. The federal government placed a tax on all photographs to raise money to pay for fighting the Civil War and required these stamps be used from August 1, 1864 to August 1, 1866. Photographers were also supposed to cancel the stamps with their name and a cancellation date which narrows down the date of a photograph even further. In practice, however, not many photographers actually added the date when canceling the stamps, but those who followed the regulation provide another very important bit of information for today's researchers.

The paper format of the carte de visite and its link with the calling card tradition also encouraged another helpful practice for modern photograph researchers that was less common with cased images. People often wrote the identities of the photograph's subjects on the front or back. Written in either ink or pencil, the presence of a name also opens the door to searches of family and census records.

Care and Preservation

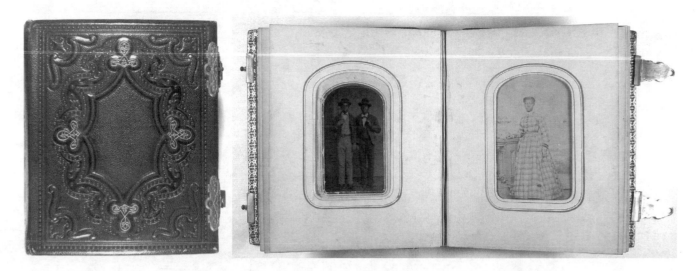

Soon after the introduction of the carte de visite format, the photograph album was invented to store and display cards. The most common had an embossed leather cover (left) with pages designed to allow the insertion of cartes de visite and similar sized tintypes.

Reasonable care of carte de visite photographs will insure their survival for generations to come. As with all early photographs, they should be kept dry and away from any extremes in heat (below 65°F) and humidity (30-40%) if possible. Much of the damage experienced by cartes de visite over the years have been from improper storage in attics and basements. They should never be exposed to direct sunlight or other sources of bright light which can cause the image on the albumen coated paper to fade. You should be very careful in the handling them since the paper can absorb dirt and oil from the skin. Transparent "archival" quality sleeves made to fit various sizes of paper photographs can be purchased (see "Additional Resources") and are strongly recommended. NEVER laminate original photographs or store them in modern photo albums with "magnetic" pages that places photographs on paper coated with an adhesive. NEVER try to clean or otherwise "restore" an original carte de visite. This should only be undertaken by a professional conservator. Excellent copies of photographs can now be made and images restored by digital means through use of the computer. These copies can then be safely framed and displayed to be shared with your family. This will place much less stress on the originals that you store in an acid free "archival" quality box in a dry, dark and safe location. If the cards are still housed in period albums, they can be left inside if they albums are in good condition. You may want to place acid free tissue paper between each page to protect the surfaces of the photographs. Cards should be removed from albums in poor condition, but be sure to note any identifications that may accompany a photograph on its album page. This could written on the back of the card with soft lead pencil (never use ink!). You may still want to save the album, regardless of its condition, to preserve the original context of the photographs. Seek the advice of the curator of prints and photographs from you state historical museum for specific recommendations for the care of your albums and photographs. Also refer to the publications in "Additional Resources" for more detailed recommendations.

Collecting Tips

Studio photographs in any early format of African Americans that interpret their work are rare and highly sought after by collectors. The unidentified woman proudly displays her new washing machine in her carte de visite (left). The unidentified sailor (right) was one of 9,596 African Americans that served in the U.S. Navy during the Civil War.

Many of the tips given for the collection of African American daguerreotypes, ambrotypes and tintypes apply to cartes de visite as well. The format also has some of its own unique criteria for collecting.

— Cartes de visite of African Americans very often exhibit condition problems. Exposure to dirt, moisture, along with tears and general neglect have damaged many of these paper photographs. But regardless of condition, they are all important and those that survive preserve the faces of a proportionally small segment of the general population from the past.

— Cartes de visite were usually purchased by the half dozen or dozen as multiple prints could be made from a glass negative. Consequently, the chances are less likely that an original paper photograph will be a totally unique "one of a kind" image like the daguerreotype, ambrotype and some tintypes. Chances are good, however, that few of the original group of cartes have survived. Since some photographers cleaned off the emulsion of the negatives to re-use the glass plates or they were broken or otherwise recycled over the years, very few of the original negatives still exist as well.

— Portraits of African American workers with their tools, firemen, and musicians are uncommon and valuable. Cartes de visite of black soldiers and sailors from the Civil War period or later are particularly in demand and can command prices that run into thousands of dollars. The identity of the soldier or sailor and the inclusion of weapons in the portrait can enhance its value as well.

Portraits of African American musicians are popular among collectors. In the carte de visite on the left, the subjects are identified on the reverse as the "Bell Boys at the Barret House, Burlington, Iowa." While one taps his tambourine, the other plays "the bones." Strong evidence is needed to support the conclusion that a subject is a slave. The young nurse with her charge (right) may have once been held in bondage, but checking the dates of operation for the Baltimore photographer shows that this carte de visite was made after the Civil War and the end of slavery. The dress of the child was also tinted red by the photographer.

— Any cartes de visite of slaves are in demand. As found with the daguerreotype and ambrotype, the portraits of nurses with children are the most common. Portraits of slaves with the adults they served are much rarer. Any studio portraits of slaves by themselves are very rare. In this case, there should be strong evidence to support the conclusion that the subject was truly a slave at the time their photograph was made.

— Cartes de visite were produced until the end of the 19th century. Later examples generally do not command the higher prices from collectors as those taken before emancipation due to the increase of the number of African Americans photographed and the greater survival rate of their images. However, unusual subject matter could enhance the image's monetary value.

— Outdoor cartes de visite in general are less common, but not as rare as those in the daguerreotype or ambrotype format. Those that picture African Americans could command high prices depending on the rarity of the subject manner and availability of the view today. Some Civil War related scenes were taken for commercial sale so they may have been reproduced in quantity.

— Cartes de visite by black photographers are always in demand with those of unusual subject matter or aesthetic quality being of greater interest. Portraits of black subjects by black photographers are particularly desirable.

The Original "UNCLE TOM."
[Rev. Josiah Henson.]

The ability to mass produce photographic prints from glass negatives was one of the great improvements of the wet-plate process. This lead to the creation of the "publicity photograph" industry to meet the public's demand for photographs of famous people of the day. The first carte de visite of an African American to be mass marketed was of Nicholas Biddle (left). Biddle was a servant to an officer of a Pennsylvania regiment that was in route to protect Washington, D.C. on April 18, 1861 after the South's attack on Fort Sumter. He was struck on the head and wounded by a brickbat while passing through Baltimore to become the first African American casualty of the Civil War. Josiah Henson (right), a former slave born in Maryland, claimed to be the model for the character Uncle Tom in Harriet Beecher Stowe's influential novel Uncle Tom's Cabin.

— Modern technology increases the problem of fake photographs with the advent of the carte de visite and other paper print formats. Color copiers along with laser and inkjet printers make forging vintage photographs tempting. Due to their high prices, photographs of African Americans along with those of Native Americans, cowboys, Civil War soldiers and baseball players are the most common fakes encountered. Beware of prints glued over the top of other card mounted photographs. The paper used to make electronic copies is usually thicker than original albumen paper and helps to unmask a fraudulent image. Examining the print with a magnifying glass may reveal the tiny parallel lines made by a color copier, the tiny dots of an ink-jet printer or the dots of a half-tone print (used to reproduce photographs in books, magazines, etc.) all of which indicate a modern copy. The best protection is a written guarantee of authenticity from a reputable dealer.

Former slave and civil rights advocate Frederick Douglass was the most photographed African American of the 19th century and his cartes de visite were widely distributed. His portrait (left) taken in Hillsdale, Michigan, was made in January 1863 while in route to Chicago, Illinois. In the later portrait (right) taken in Vermont just a few years later, we see that Douglass had removed his beard while his hair became grayer. Isabella Baumfree (below) was born a slave in New York and was freed when slavery was abolished there in 1828. After experiencing a spiritual revelation, she adopted the name "Sojourner Truth" and sold her carte de visite "shadows" to raise money to live on as she campaigned against slavery and for women's rights. Cartes de visite like these are avidly sought by collectors.

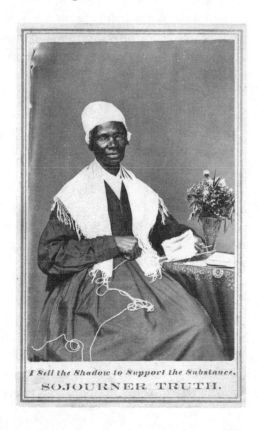

Focal Point: **Selling the "Slaves from New Orleans"**

This carte de visite is No. 6 in a series published by New York photographer Charles Paxson in 1864 of former slaves (left to right) Rosina (Rosa) Downs, Rebecca Huger, Charles Taylor, and Wilson Chinn. It was stated on the reverse that net proceeds from its sale were to be "devoted to the education of the Colored People in the department of the Gulf, now under the command of Major General Banks."

One of the reasons for the quick success of the wet-plate process was the ability to economically mass produce thousands of paper prints from a single glass plate negative. This helped fuel the publicity picture industry as photographers and their publishers sought to capitalize on the public's demand to see and own the photographs of notables of the day. This also opened up the door to the use of photographs as a vehicle for fundraising as interest groups sought to promote their beliefs. When the Civil War broke out in 1861, the issue of a state's right to secede from the Union, and not slavery, was considered the immediate cause of the conflict. Abolitionists recognized the opportunity presented by photography to promote their campaign for the destruction of slavery and help those that suffered from its practice.

When New Orleans fell to Union forces in the spring of 1862, Major-General Nathaniel Banks ordered the creation of schools to educate the slaves under his control. Philip Bacon who served as Assistant Superintendent of Freedman, visited New York in 1864 with a group of his students seeking to raise funds for the operation of the school and to show the public the horrors of the slavery. His group of eight freed slaves were photographed individually and in groups several times creating an extensive and dramatic record to be used as anti-slavery propaganda.

Among the most widely circulated cartes de visite of this group, the four seen in this group were among the most photographed. The three children (from left to right) were Rosina Downs, Rebecca Huger, Charles Taylor along with the older Wilson Chinn on the far right. Six years old Rosina Downs was described in *Harper's Weekly* as "a fair child, with blond complexion and silky hair" whose father was in the rebel army and her mother, "a bright mulatto," lived in poor hut in New Orleans. Eleven year old Rebecca Huger had been "a slave in her father's house, the special attendant of a girl a little older than herself." She was described as appearing to be "perfectly white" and that her "complexion, hair and features show not the slightest trace of Negro blood." Eight year old Charles Taylor had a mother who had been sold twice as a slave, the first time to a slave trader by his father living in Virginia. It was reported that "his complexion is very fair, his hair light and silky." His mother was described as a mulatto who had seen her daughter sold off to live in Texas and a son still held as slave in Virginia. The idea that these fair haired children could have ever been held in bondage was shocking to Northerners who did not fully understand the consequences of southern law that based the decision on whether or not a child was a slave on the mother's and not the father's legal standing.

Wilson Chinn was also an effective weapon for the abolitionist cause. Being "about sixty years old" (official records of slave births were not required), he had been sold to Volsey B. Marmillion, a sugar planter who had the custom of branding his slaves. On his forehead, Wilson bore "VBM" burned into his flesh. It was reported that of the 105 slaves belonging to Marmillion that Wilson had escaped along with, "thirty had been branded like cattle with a hot iron, four of them on the forehead, and others on the breast or arm." Other photographs taken of Wilson showed him with his branding prominently displayed surrounded by implements used to torture slaves while he modeled a bulky "slave collar" designed to prevent a slave from running away.

As an interesting comment on the racism encountered in the North at that time, *Harper's* reported that the three children, along with Mr. Bacon, had earlier checked into the St. Lawrence Hotel in Philadelphia in December. Within a few hours, Bacon was notified by the landlord that they had to leave since the proprietor had found out about the children's slave background and "they must therefore be colored persons, and he kept a hotel for white people." Bacon had to take these children to another hotel in the "City of Brotherly Love" where they were found not to be so offensive.

**WILSON CHINN, a Branded Slave from Louisiana.
Also exhibiting Instruments of Torture
used to punish Slaves.**
Photographed by KIMBALL, 477 Broadway, N.Y
Entered according to Act of Congress, in the year 1863, by
GEO. H. HANKS, in the Clerk's Office of the United States for
the Southern District of New-York.

Escaped slave Wilson Chinn posed wearing a slave collar along with other "Instruments of Torture used to punish Slaves." The branded initials of his former owner are seen on his forehead. Original cartes de visite of this famous portrait command high prices among collectors.

A pair of unidentified street entertainers brought a smile to a little girl in this Pennsylvania cabinet card ca. 1890. The circumstances behind the taking of this portrait have been lost in time. We can almost be certain that the clothing of the boys were not costumes and that their future held little promise of formal education.

5

THE CABINET CARD

With the end of the Civil War came the final end to the "peculiar institution" of slavery. Over 4 million African Americans were now free to determine their own destinies as well as create their own legacies. Those previously held in bondage were now at least free to visit the photographers studio to record themselves as free individuals no longer dependent on the whim of an owner deciding their access to immortality.

The popularity of the carte de visite during the Civil War had filled photo albums in many of the nation's parlors with a flood of images of the war along with family, friends, and notables of the day. Fearing a slackening in demand for portraits since the war's end also ended the need for large numbers of soldiers to record themselves, something new to stimulate the photographic business was eagerly sought. The solution came from England where a photographer there is credited with introducing a new photographic format that dominated studio portraiture until the end of the century. This new photographic format was named the "cabinet card" and it was used extensively to record the faces of 19th century African Americans.

The cabinet card format was similar to the earlier carte de visite in that a paper photographic print was pasted on a cardboard mount. But in this case, the mount was approximately 4 ¼ x 6 ½ inches with the print being approximately 4 x 5 ½ inches — almost twice the size of the carte de visite photographs. Photographic albums that had pages with larger windows to view this new sized photograph were soon produced. These albums, that were generally larger than those most commonly used with the carte de visite, had covers of plush velvet, embossed leather, celluloid, or even silver plate. They also often included pages designed to hold the smaller cartes de visite or tintypes as well since these also remained in production during the period.

To obtain a cabinet photograph, subjects still visited the photographer's studio for a sitting. Cost ranged from about $2.00 to as much as $6.00 a dozen. Wet-plate glass negatives were still used in the camera though commercially manufactured gelatin dry plates that offered greater ease in processing and faster exposure times became widely employed in the 1880s. After exposure, developing, and fixing, the negative was coated with varnish to protect the emulsion. Then a new practice emerged, made possible and necessary by the use of larger negatives, and rapidly gained popularity among studios. The negative was now retouched by the photographer to enhance the subject's appearance. Wrinkles and blemishes could be erased, hair smoothed, and the overall appearance of the subject enhanced. It also became stylish to manipulate negatives or prints as well to produce a flattering "soft focus" effect. Printing of photographs from the negatives was still made by exposure to sunlight and the resulting photographs were fixed, toned, dried, trimmed and mounted on cardboard. Another new practice appeared in which the photograph's surface was coated with glazes and burnished by running the card between a pair of polished rollers. As time progressed, card mounts were produced in a variety of colors and edge finishes and photographers' imprints on the front and back became more elaborate. The resulting product, coupled with flattering poses and fancy studio props, could make even the most homely subject appear attractive and elegant.

Care and Preservation

The red velvet covered photograph album (left) is typical of those produced after the Civil War to house the new cabinet card style along with earlier cartes de visite. Photographs were slipped into pockets (right) for storage and display. To remove them, carefully insert the blade of a blunt knife under the card and gently slide it out to avoid damaging the album page. If the album is in overall good condition, you might want to leave the photographs in place and lay sheets of acid free tissue paper between pages to protect them.

Like other paper photographs, cabinet cards are fragile and subject to tearing, staining, and mold if improperly handled and stored. Cards should be kept in an environment that avoids the extremes of temperature and humidity and out of direct sunlight that can cause photographs to fade. Though a relative humidity of 30-40% and a temperature that does not exceed 65° F is the recommended museum environment for all 19th century paper photographs, this may be difficult to apply in the home. Just remember- if you are feeling uncomfortable, your vintage photographs are as well! And never store them in the attic or basement. Also avoid keeping them in an area that is exposed to cigarette smoke or the fumes of paints and other harmful chemicals. An attempt should always be made to store these precious pieces of our heritage in a way that does not bring them further harm. Use archival certified boxes made of acid free cardboard to store individual photographs and albums. Transparent archival sleeves should be purchased to house individual cards. (See "Additional Resources" for dealers in archival supplies.) Acid free tissue paper can be placed between the pages of albums to protect cabinet cards. Removal of cards from albums can be difficult and the pages easily torn. Use a flat blade to slip under card mounts to slide them from page slots. If cards are permanently removed, be sure to make note of any information about the card that may be written on the album page. Make a separate tag to include with the photograph that could be slipped behind it in its protective sleeve or use a soft lead pencil to print the information on the back of the card. Restoration should only be undertaken by a professional conservator. Contact the curator of prints and photographs at your state historical society for recommendations. Cards can be digitally copied and enhanced often with remarkable results. Photographic prints can then be made for framing and distribution to family members.

Tips for Collecting

No matter how humble, 19th century Americans, both black and white, were proud of their work and turned to the photographer's studio to make "occupational portraits" which are popular among collectors. With the end of slavery, the cabinet card frequently recorded those endeavors of African American as well. The unidentified nurse (left) must have been a valued member of a Baltimore family. Two waiters (center) proudly posed in their uniforms with a table covering that perhaps symbolized their now forgotten restaurant. The housekeeper (right) wore her pressed apron and added a broom to interpret her life's work for her dignified portrait.

— Cabinet cards of African American often have conditions from improper storage and exposure to moisture. Rare subject matter can still cause the photograph to be highly valued.

— Cabinet cards of blacks are more common than daguerreotypes, ambrotypes, and Civil War era tintypes and cartes de visite. Identities of subjects enhances value as well. Anonymous but attractive portraits, particular of young women, children and infants are collectible since many photographers competed to create portraits that could be considered to be works of art.

— Any examples made by African American photographers are desirable and those that picture black subjects are particularly rare and highly sought. Cabinet cards from J.P. Ball's studio as well as the Goodridge gallery are in demand. The work of other lesser known black photographers remain to be discovered and collected as well.

— Uncommon subject matter such as occupational portraits, musicians, famous people, and outdoor scenes are desirable. Post mortem portraits of the dead are also uncommon of African Americans and in demand.

— Portraits of black soldiers are valuable, particularly if they are members of the western "Buffalo Soldier" cavalry and infantry regiments. Cards signed by western photographers will be a clue to look for. Soldiers posed with their firearms are even more desirable and any individual and/or unit identification further enhances the cabinet card's value.

— Family albums that have remained intact over the years are uncommon and every effort should be made to keep all of the pictures together, particularly if the subjects in the cabinet cards are identified and/or if the family is known. Unfortunately, it is common practice for cards to be removed from albums and sold separately by antique dealers, especially if a particular card has unusual subject matter which commands high prices among collectors.

Cabinet cards of African Americans in the military are eagerly sought by collectors, especially those that record true "buffalo soldiers" out west. The portrait of the unidentified trooper (left) was a member of the 10th U.S. Cavalry taken at Fort Assinniboine in Montana. The unidentified American sailor (right) stopped in Hong Kong to have his cabinet card made.

This cabinet card of two unidentified hunting partners is a study in contrasting wealth. The spotting is due to negligence over the years and is permanent damage.

The larger size of the cabinet card and competition among photographers to make artistic portraits created a wide spectrum of interesting work recording African Americans. An unidentified woman (top left) recorded her religious devotion in a Baltimore studio as did an Oblate Sister of Providence (top right), the first congregation of African American nuns in the United States. Physical deformities (bottom left) were sometimes emphasized rather than hidden in 19th century portraits since they defined the uniqueness of the individual or were used as medical illustrations. African Americans also adopted the latest in fashion as well as seen in the portrait taken in Georgia of the young boy (bottom center) wearing his "Little Lord Fountleroy" style inspired by Frances Hodgson Burnett's story of the same name. An elderly man (bottom right), possibly a former slave, proudly posed for a Pennsylvania photographer with a boy that may have been his grandson and would not know firsthand the horrors of the "peculiar institution."

Elizabeth Fairfax sold this cabinet card to raise money to support herself and her children. For her portrait, she wore a silk badge for the General N.B. Baker Post of the Grand Army of the Republic organized in Clinton, Iowa, for men who had fought in the Civil War.

Focal Point: Searching for a Civil War Veteran

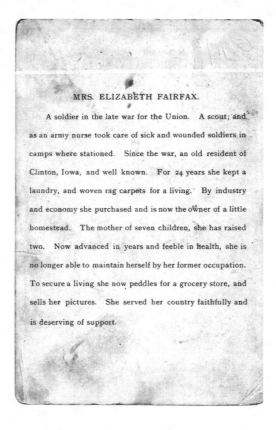

MRS. ELIZABETH FAIRFAX.

A soldier in the late war for the Union. A scout; and as an army nurse took care of sick and wounded soldiers in camps where stationed. Since the war, an old resident of Clinton, Iowa, and well known. For 24 years she kept a laundry, and woven rag carpets for a living. By industry and economy she purchased and is now the owner of a little homestead. The mother of seven children, she has raised two. Now advanced in years and feeble in health, she is no longer able to maintain herself by her former occupation. To secure a living she now peddles for a grocery store, and sells her pictures. She served her country faithfully and is deserving of support.

On the back of her cabinet card, Elizabeth Fairfax told her story.

A number of years ago, a cabinet card was offered for sale in a mail auction that was very intriguing. It was a portrait taken in Clinton, Iowa, of an African American woman prominently wearing a ribbon for the H.B. Baker Post of the Grand Army of the Republic. Founded in 1866, the G.A.R. was a fraternal organization open to all men who had served in the Union Army during the Civil War. People of that time would not have expected to see any woman, particularly one who was black, wearing one of their badges for a formal studio photograph taken in Iowa or anywhere else. On the back of the card was printed information that offered some explanation. The subject of the photograph was Mrs. Elizabeth Fairfax, "a soldier in the late war for the Union," who was then a resident of Clinton where she worked as a washwoman and struggled to raise her two children. Since she was a widow, Elizabeth sold her photographs to raise money for the support of her family. This was an untold story from the Civil War and its uncovering serves as a model for researching identified photographs.

The first place to look were the census records (www.ancestry.com) to see if Mrs. Fairfax could be located. A quick search turned up her entry in the 1880 Iowa census (she is also listed in the 1870 census) as a resident in Clinton, and it is possible to view the actual census page with her information online. Elizabeth was listed as a widowed mulatto female, age 36, born in Tennessee, occupation of washwoman with two children: Mary, age 18, and Abraham, age 12. (The birthplace of her children's deceased father was identified as being England.) Having established her residence and verifying some of the information

This is part of the entry for Elizabeth Fairfax and her two children from the 1880 census. The mark to the left of her occupation indicates that she was a widow. Unfortunately, there is no mention of the identity of her husband in any records.

given on the back of her photograph, the next step was to find Elizabeth's obituary in a local newspaper. Though the time and place of her death were unknown, Clinton, Iowa, was the obvious place to look. Access to genealogical information from Clinton seemed daunting since it is about 900 miles away from the author's home in Baltimore, Maryland, but the power of the internet overcame the distance.

On the website for the Iowa State Historical Society is a list of people who work for a fee doing genealogical research. One person on the list lived in Clinton, Iowa, and when contacted, she agreed to help with the search. She soon found the key to uncovering Elizabeth's story.

In many states, extraordinarily dedicated genealogists explore the graveyards that dot the country side recording the information found on tombstones for publication in compiled indexes. Using the index for the Clinton County cemeteries in Iowa (published by the Clinton County Gateway Genealogical Society), the researcher found Elizabeth Fairfax's grave in Clinton and the date of her death — April 18, 1908. Armed with this information, she then turned to the microfilm for *The Clinton Daily Herald* and the story behind the photograph was revealed.

In the April 22, 1908 issue, it was announced that "Aunt Lizzie" was found dead in her small cottage by Clinton police. The former slave had been a camp servant to the Twenty-sixth Iowa Regiment during the Civil War while they were stationed in the South at Vicksburg, Mississippi. At the end of the conflict, she had followed the regiment back to Iowa and established her home there. Though she was never officially employed as a nurse, veterans recounted that she probably assisted with the sick and wounded as she worked washing and cooking for the men in the regiment. After the war, she worked as a laundress and walked the Clinton streets selling matches and chewing gum from a basket as she cheerfully remarked "God bless you honey" to her customers. Her obituary also mentioned that she never missed an opportunity to attend a reunion of veterans or march with them on Memorial Day. The commander of the General H.B. Baker G.A.R. Post ordered all members who could turn out for her funeral, and the A.M.E. Methodist Church was filled to capacity the next day to mourn her death. Elizabeth was buried in the section of the graveyard reserved for Civil War soldiers and veterans and a Grand Army of the Republic marker stands at attention today next to her grave. Through the use of technology and the work of dedicated genealogists, another forgotten African American story has been rediscovered.

HONORED BURIAL FOR 'AUNT LIZZIE'

Veterans of the Civil War Turn Out to Pay Tribute of Respect to the Memory of Aged Colored Woman.

MANY WHITE PEOPLE ATTEND THE OBSEQUIES

Funeral Services Held at the African Methodist Episcopal Church Thursday Afternoon, Followed by Interment in Springdale.

"Aunt Lizzie" Fairfax the friend of the old soldiers, was honored by the veterans of Clinton yesterday when

The Clinton Daily Herald *from April 24, 1908 (above) carried the story of the funeral held for Elizabeth "Aunt Lizzie" Fairfax. She was buried in the section of the local cemetery reserved for those who had served during the Civil War. Today, a Grand Army of the Republic marker is found placed next to her tombstone (bottom). Her son Abraham, who had died earlier in 1901, is buried nearby.*

This enlargement from one side of a stereoview was taken of an unidentified African American man standing on Cathedral Street in Baltimore, Maryland. Published in 1858 as part of "Langenheim's American Stereoscopic Views," this may be the first stereoview that shows an African American outdoors in the United States. Since the city had the largest free black population in the country at that time, further evidence would be needed to determine whether or not this individual was a slave.

STEREOVIEWS

Langenheim stereoview published in 1858 of Cathedral Street in Baltimore, Maryland.

The principles of binocular vision that allows us to see in three dimensions were discovered before the invention of photography. The appearance of this new medium, however, made it possible to apply this knowledge to its fullest potential. Though used with the earlier daguerreotype process, this three-dimensional photography, known as stereography, was joined with the wet-plate process to become a major source of parlor entertainment and education for Americans during the 19th and early 20th centuries. No Victorian parlor was considered complete without a stack of stereoscopic cards that cost a few pennies or more each and a special stereoviewer that enabled people to see their world with a unique perspective.

In this format, a camera was used that had two lenses (or a single lens camera that was moved to make two exposures) spaced about two inches apart approximating the distance between a person's eyes. A pair of negative exposures were made on the light sensitive glass plate from which positive paper prints were contact printed. These prints were trimmed and mounted on a piece of rectangular cardboard approximately $3\,{}^{5}\!/_{16}$ x 7 inches in size. When the card is observed through a special viewer that allows the eyes to see only one side of the image pair, the brain merges the two perspectives to produce a three-dimensional image. During much of the 19th century, the ability to photo-mechanically reproduce photographs in print through the use of tiny dots in the halftone process (like that used in this book) did not yet exist. Consequently, the ability to mass produce paper prints from the glass negatives created the unlimited potential for enterprising photographers to capitalize on the public's desire to see the world literally "in depth."

Cameras with two lenses (left) were developed early on with lenses that imitated the spacing between the eyes needed to achieve depth perception. When stereocards printed from glass or film negatives were viewed through a stereoscope (right), a three-dimensional image is created.

The production of stereoviews quickly became a major industry with the start of the Civil War as Americans clamored to see the stage and the faces of the cast of characters that were part of this national drama. Photographers were sent into the field to record the camps and battlefields with their two lensed cameras, and negatives were exposed to produce the stereocards sold to the home front. After the end of the conflict, stereographers sought out scenes world-wide that could be sold to the public until the decline in interest after World War I.

Subject Matter

The vast numbers of stereoscopic cards produced were usually outdoor scenic views and interiors when sufficient lighting was available. They were usually taken by professional photographers and reproduced for sale to the public. Stereography was limited in its use for general studio portraiture unless the subject was prominent enough that their stereocard could be sold. The value in stereography was recording images that the public wanted to see and ultimately buy. The outdoor perspective that enhanced the three-dimensional effect made this the ideal format to satisfy the market.

Stereoviews depicting African Americans represent a significant portion of stereoviews published during the 19th and early 20th centuries. The Civil War and the struggle to end slavery made white Americans very curious about those that had lived and worked in the South as slaves. The stereoviews published to meet this demand usually fall into one of three categories. Stereoviews that recorded blacks engaged in the spectrum of southern agricultural activities, usually relating to cotton production, were popular subjects throughout this era. Other occupations for blacks were also captured by Southern photographers like O.P. Havens as well. Views of their humble and often primitive homes were frequently published. Judging by their captions, some of these views were subtly racist and filled many northern or southern purchasers with a sense of superiority. However, a major category of stereoviews with black themes were those with overt racist intent. Hundreds of subjects were published that demeaned African Americans through the use of stereotypes and humor that fed on the racism of "Jim

Cabinet size stereoview of chimney sweeps published by Wilson and Havens in Savannah, Georgia. These boys probably faced a grim future of work with little educational opportunity.

Crow" America. As distasteful as these are today, they represent a significant part of our photographic legacy and a subject for cataloguing and study. A third and much smaller category of stereoviews are those that recorded important African Americans and their notable achievements. Portraits of people such as Booker T. Washington and boxer Jack Johnson joined views of black soldiers from the Spanish-American War through World War I to give a more positive, but limited view of African American society. But regardless of their intent, even the most racist stereoviews recorded the faces of many African Americans of the past that may have otherwise never been photographed.

Stereoview published by the Keystone View Company of an arithmetic class at Tuskegee Institute founded by Booker T. Washington to bring education and job training to former slaves and their descendants.

Dating Stereocards

Curved mount stereoview published by Underwood & Underwood in 1899 of troops who fought in Cuba during Spanish-American War.

Several clues can help in dating stereocards. Some cards carry a copyright date or the descriptive caption may also include a date for the event recorded. Clues within the stereo photograph may help date it as well, particularly with changing city scapes where distinct buildings are added or removed from the scene. Caution must be taken though because some earlier views were published at later times such as the Civil War stereoviews of Brady/Anthony and Alexander Gardner. Stereocards can often be dated by the changing format styles as the years of activity for the publisher. The following should help you determine when a stereoview was made.

Sizes/ Formats: $3\frac{5}{16}$ x 7 inches flat cardboard mounts with square corners emerged in the later 1850s. The size remained standard though colors of card mounts vary with publishers. Rounded corners for mounts became the standard after the Civil War. Around 1874, the "cabinet" size was introduced that was 7 inches wide by 4 to 4 ½ inches tall. The smaller $3\frac{5}{16}$ x 7 inch format still remained the most commonly used size.

Curved or "warped" mounts: introduced in 1882 by stereo publisher B.W. Kilburn. Most publishers switched to the curved mount by 1890.

Lithoprints: stereoviews produced through the halftone printing system that uses small dots. Color printed "lithos" were introduced in 1898 with major black & white series issued after about 1904.

Tax Stamps: like other photographs, stereoviews were subject to taxation during the Civil War from August 1, 1864 until August 1, 1866. Revenue stamps were pasted on the back of the card mount.

Stereoview published E. & H.T. Anthony & Co. of U.S. Colored Troops sitting next to a bombproof quarters at Dutch Gap, on the James River in Virginia during the Civil War. Though taken in 1864, the label on the reverse has the 591 Broadway address for the publishers where they were located after 1869. This indicates that the actual stereoview was manufactured after that time.

Labels: Labeling ranges from script identifications of photographer and/or locations, letterpress identifications/ copyright notices on the front of mounts, and paper labels or textual descriptions on the reverse as well. The Anthony Co. was most prolific publisher of stereoviews made during the Civil War and featured the work of Mathew Brady and his photographers along with Alexander Gardner. The following is a brief guide to the dating of many of these views that are known to include African Americans:

— "Published by E. Anthony, 501 Broadway, New-York." Edward Anthony moves his photographic business to 501 Broadway in May 1860.

— "Published by E. & H.T. Anthony & Co./ American and Foreign Stereoscopic Emporium, 501 Broadway, New York." Business name adds Edward's brother Henry T. Anthony on July 9, 1862.

— "From Gardner's Gallery, corner of 7th and D streets, Washington, D.C./ Negative by Alex. Gardner./ E.& H.T. Anthony , 501 Broadway, New York, Wholesale Agents." Alexander Gardner separates from Brady and opens his Washington, D.C. gallery at this location in May 1863. Some of his later labels carry this same location's street number of "511 Seventh St." in 1864 and adds a gallery address of 332 Pennsylvania Ave in 1865. Gardner maintains a Washington, D.C. gallery until September 1867. Photographs with a 921 Pennsylvania Ave. studio address were printed after the Civil War.

— "Published by E. & H.T. Anthony & Co.,/ Emporium of American and Foreign Stereoscopic Views, Chromos and Albums,/ 591 Broadway, opposite Metropolitan Hotel, New-York." The Anthony's move to the 591 Broadway location in 1869.

— "Taylor & Huntington, No. 2 State St., Hartford, Conn." and "The War Photograph & Exhibition Company, No. 21 Linden Place, Hartford, Conn." In 1884, the Anthony collection of Brady's negatives along with negatives from Alexander Gardner were purchased by John C. Taylor in Hartford, Connecticut. Taylor proceeded to published stereoviews into the 1890s, mostly in the cabinet size, under the "Taylor & Huntington" and "The War Photograph & Exhibition Company" labels. Taylor sold the collection in 1907.

Other frequently encountered publishers of stereoviews with African Americans:
— Barnard, George N.: 1873 – late 1880 for South Carolina stereoviews with Barnard imprint.
— Bell, C.M. and F.A., Bell Brothers, Washington, D.C.: 1865–1875
— Chase, William M.: 1869–1890
— Jarvis, James F., 1870s–1890s
— Keystone View Co.: 1892–1964
— Kilburn Brothers: 1865–1877
— B.W. Kilburn: 1877–1909
— Littleton View Co.: 1880s–1897
— Underwood & Underwood: about 1882–1921
— Wilson, J. N.: 1860s–1870s; partnered with O.P. Havens in late 1870s.

Flat mount stereocard in 1871 by James Black in Boston, Massachusetts, of the Jubilee Singers from Fisk University. The troup toured the United Sates and Europe to raise funds for their school as they performed "slave songs" and received international acclaim. The spotting is permanent damage caused by inappropriate handling and storage.

Care and Preservation

Stereoviews were made to be handled and often exhibit problems with soiling, chips to mounts, creases and tears. Any attempt to restore them should be left to an experienced conservator. As with other early paper photographic formats, transparent archival sleeves are available for the both the standard and cabinet size mounts. Acid free cardboard boxes can also be purchased to store them (see "Additional Resources"). They should be kept in a stable environment away from extremes in temperature and humidity. A temperature of 65° F and a relative humidity of 30-40% are considered ideal. Digital means can be used to restore and reproduce valuable stereocards used for frequent handling and public display. Inexpensive plastic viewers and reproductions of the antique viewers are also available for viewing these images in 3-D.

Historically important flat mount stereoview published by Bell & Bro., Washington, D.C. of the "Freedman's Village" on what is today Arlington National Cemetery. Established by the federal government during the Civil War in 1863 for freed slaves who moved to the capital, the village provided housing, schools, medical care, and church services until it was closed in 1887.

Collecting Tips

— Stereo daguerreotypes or ambrotypes were expensive and are uncommon and much fewer were made than the more common singular portraits. Any that record African American subjects are extremely rare and valuable.

— Any stereoviews that record slaves are rare and important. Strong evidence needs to support this conclusion since numerous stereoviews were taken of southern blacks soon after their liberation by the Union Army during the Civil War. African Americans pictured in these views may have been slaves at one time and the lifestyle depicted may well have reflected the slave experience, but stereoviews of actual slaves are very rare. Stereoviews produced in the Confederacy that picture slaves are also very rare and important.

— As with other photographic formats, stereoviews many have condition problems. Rare views even in poor condition, particularly those that recorded significant places and events by less frequently encountered publishers, are important. Digital restoration can often correct problems to produce a usable reproduction.

— Stereoviews by amateur photographers that include African Americans are very rare. These may be recognized by hand written labels on the back, but some professional photographers used this method for small edition issues as well.

— Any stereoview by an African American photographer is exceedingly rare. None have been found made by the well-known black photographers in the 19th century.

— Half-tone lithoviews sometimes feature black subjects, but are generally in lesser demand than stereoviews made with actual photographic prints.

— Over the years, both reproductions of important stereocards and intentional fakes meant to deceive buyers have been made. Advances in digital reproduction and printing make this a continual problem, particularly when buying something online that you cannot examine first-hand. If purchasing expensive views, deal with reputable dealers who will give you a written guarantee of authenticity.

Cabinet card size amateur stereoview of the caretaker of George Washington's Tomb at Mount Vernon taken June 26, 1899. The unidentified man may have been a descendent of Washington's slaves. Amateur stereoviews are uncommon and those that feature African Americans are very rare.

140. Washington's Tomb, Mt. Vernon, Va.

Another view of George Washington's tomb keeper; this stereoview was published as a color lithographic stereoview. "Litho" stereoviews were printed by the half-tone process that uses tiny dots to make a picture. Though in color, these stereoviews do not command the prices of those printed directly from actual negatives.

This stereocard on a curved mount published in 1904 by Underwood & Underwood is an example of the large number with racist subject matter that were published during 19th and early 20th centuries. Though they are generally not sought after by many collectors, they document stereotypes and attitudes prevalent in their era and cannot be ignored.

Keystone stereoview on a curved mount of the famous 369th Regiment "Harlem's Own" marching in New York City in 1919 after the end of World War I. Stereoviews of black soldiers from any period are sought by collectors.

Photo postcard by H.M. Bryan that has written on its back "To dear Miss Eakins, From Victoria with love."
Considering that Victoria still chose to pose wrapped in the American flag during the era in which she faced "Jim
Crow" segregation laws makes this portrait even more historically compelling.

PHOTO POSTCARDS

A technological explosion at the dawn of the 20th century forever changed photography and the picture taking process. New inexpensive cameras using flexible roll film instead of glass plates, advances in commercially produced photographic printing paper and the advent of the light bulb for printing helped to remove photography solely from the hands of the professional or serious amateur to mainstream America. For a modest cost, anyone could now shoot pictures and the photo printing businesses cropping up around the country provided citizens with cheap film processing and printing. A new format appeared at this time that became extremely popular recording many African Americans as well as others well into the 1920s. This new style of photograph was called the photo postcard.

The development of the photo postcard format was helped by expanded services and new rules adopted by the U.S. Postal Service. By 1906, Rural Free Delivery routes had been established that brought mail delivery to Americans still living on the many family farms that dotted the rural landscape. No longer did farmers have to wait until they got to town to collect their letters and packages. Earlier, the Post Office set a reduced rate for the mailing of postcards to one cent though it was stipulated that one side of the card could be used only for the address of the recipient. Any messages had to written on the front. Nevertheless, the rage for sending colorful printed postcards that had started in Europe quickly spread to America. In 1902, the Eastman Kodak Company introduced photographic paper the size of postcards (3 ¼ x 5 ½ in.) that could be contact printed directly from the film negatives. The sensitivity of these faster papers was so improved that sunlight was no longer needed for this operation. An electric light or even gaslight could be used for exposure. The following year Kodak introduced the No. 3A Folding Pocket Kodak camera which made postcard size film negatives. Then the Postal Office soon changed their rules to also allow messages to be written on the addressed side of the postcard. The making of photo postcards exploded in America like nothing seen since the days of "cartemania" with the introduction of the carte de visite just 40 years earlier. As the public quickly embraced the new style of photography, many professional photographers adopted the format as well. They offered this new style in their studios and set out, much like photographers during the Civil War, to record their communities as they captured moments of time that they then offered for sale to the public. These new processes also opened up the ranks of the professionals to African Americans as black owned and operated photography studios sprang up largely in urban black communities.

New style photo albums were manufactured to house the photo and colorfully printed postcards that Americans now received in the mail. The most common had an embossed cover made of black cardboard that contained sheets of heavy black paper to which the cards could be glued. Some styles had die cut slots cut in the paper so each of the corners of the card could

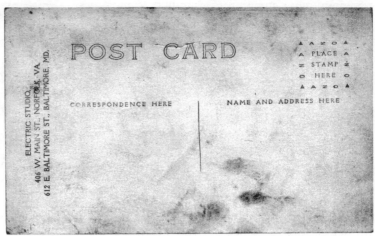

A No. 3 Folding Pocket Kodak camera sits on the table in a photo postcard portrait (left) of Elmer Carroll. After March 1, 1907, the Post Office allowed messages along with addresses on postcards and the "divided back" format appeared. In 1904, Kodak added "AZO" postcard stock that was identified in the "Place Stamp Here" block for postage. Commercial photographers sometimes added their names too.

be tucked in to secure it. Often people used white ink to write in captions, comments and other identification that provide us today with a rich record of a time long since passed. This new form of the family photo album won quick acceptance among many, including African Americans, who were now able to freely record their world with their own personal vision without depending solely on the help of a professional photographer.

One of the beauties of the photo postcard is the information that often accompanies it that helps in the card's interpretation. Based on a format that encouraged writing, cards often have comments written by the sender about the people and places seen in the picture. Some of these can be very candid and humorous even years later. Since these were made to be mailed, the presence of cancelled postage stamp also adds a place and a date to the photograph. Unmailed and otherwise undated photo cards can be dated by the style of printing and layout used on the reverse and the designs used to show where the postage stamp should be placed (see "Additional Resources" for help). Commercially produced views often have the location of an outdoor scene and possibly a date added by the photographer. Of all the forms of photographs ever produced, photo postcards as a group are the most informative about the people and the times they recorded.

Care and Preservation

Being paper photographs, photo postcards are subject to many of the problems faced by other earlier formats. Though they are relatively stable like earlier paper photographs, they are still subject to being torn, fading from the direct sunlight, destroyed by exposure extreme heat and moisture and general deterioration over time due to environmental assault. The gelatin silver paper used for photo postcards is also susceptible to "silver mirroring" seen when the surface of the photograph appears to have a silvery sheen when

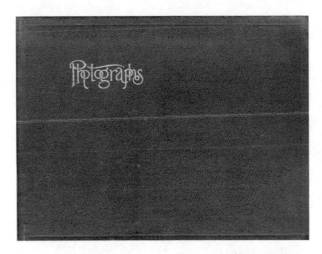

Postcard albums popular during the first three decades of the early 1900s were usually rectangular in shape with heavy embossed paper covers (left) and black pages. White ink was often used for caption writing. Acid free tissue paper should be placed between pages to preserve the photographs.

rotated in the light. This is caused by chemical changes that cannot be stopped. Storage in a low humidity environment will help to slow down this deterioration. Transparent archival sleeves are available in the post card size (see "Additional Resources" for suppliers) to protect cards during handling and storage. But it is critical to keep the humidity level low (30-50%) to prevent the gelatin surface of the photo paper from swelling and adhering to the plastic. Acid free cardboard boxes are available for storage of cards and albums. Acid free tissue paper should also be placed between pages of albums to protect photo post cards that have been mounted in albums. Cards can also be stored in binders with transparent pages that have pockets that allow the viewing and display of cards without handling them. However, make sure that all of the materials that come into close contact with your photo postcard are acid free and approved for archival use. NEVER use transparent tape to repair cards. NEVER laminate them and NEVER use "magnetic" photo album pages for storage. The adhesives used on the pages and the plastic cover can damage the photographs! Collections should be kept in an area with cool temperatures and low humidity. NEVER store photographs in attics or basements. Storage in those locations over the years has caused much of the damage that old photographs suffer from today. Seek the help of a professional museum curator or conservator for an evaluation of photographs and specific recommendations for their care.

Tips for Collecting

The collecting of photo postcards has been a very active market for many years and started as a specialty among general postcard collecting. Depending on the subject matter, some cards can command prices in the thousands of dollars. Albums of photo postcards can also command high prices as well. The following tips should help guide you in the evaluation of these photographs.

— Like other photographs, photo postcards of African American are likely to have conditions problems. Prints may be stained, torn, and/or water damaged. Albums may have also suffered abuse and neglect as well. But

Almost 400,000 African Americans served in the U.S. Army during World War I and their portraits are highly sought by collectors today. An unidentified young soldier (left) was congratulated by his father or grandfather who could have seen service during the Civil War. Walter William posed proudly with an outdated "Krag" rifle for his portrait at Camp Meade, Maryland, in August 1918 taken by Edward Herbener.

these images are still important and the value of the subject recorded may well outweigh condition problems. Digital restoration can rescue many cards previously thought to be lost.

— Due to the wider availability of the new and inexpensive photographic technology, photo postcards of black subjects are more common than earlier formats. Interesting subject matter will largely determine collecting value.

— Photo postcards were produced from a negative which has probably been lost or destroyed. However, prints could have been made in large numbers so images in this format may not have the "one of a kind" quality of the earlier daguerreotypes, ambrotypes, or tintypes.

— Commercial photographers sometimes stamped their names on the back of their cards to advertise their studios. Those operated by African American photographers are very collectible and their portraits of black Americans are particularly desirable. However, much work needs to be done to identify these studios since no complete record of 20th century black photography businesses yet exists. This creates the unique opportunity to identify and collect a significant collection of their work before it is widely discovered.

— Photo postcards of black baseball teams and players are highly valued, particularly those relating to the Negro Leagues.

The collection of early photographs, including photo postcards, for their artistic quality still presents opportunity for the savvy collector. Though the identities of the subjects, location, and the photographer were not recorded for this photo postcard (above), the portrait is still an outstanding composition worthy of a place in any collection.

Photo postcards of popular entertainers such as Josephine Baker (left) are in demand among collectors. Numerous portraits of Baker exist and most were published in Europe to promote her shows in Paris. Occupational portraits of African Americans (center) are desirable in any early photograph though they may be more common as photo postcards due the format's low cost and wide availability. Photography galleries operated by African Americans during this era still remain to be discovered and their work collected and studied. A Baltimore bride (right) was recorded in 1933 in Penn's Studio on Pennsylvania Avenue in Baltimore, Maryland. The city's famous Washington Monument was painted on the backdrop seen to the right of the lady.

Andrew Beard Negro inventor.

Portraits of less widely known but significant African Americans still remain to be discovered by collectors. Andrew Jackson Beard, a former slave, was an inventor credited with two patents for improved plows, one of which he posed with for his portrait. He also received a patent in 1897 for his most important invention, an automatic coupler for attaching railroad cars together.

— Interesting subject matter will always increase the value of photographs. Blacks seen in different roles such as police and fire personnel, nurses, or soldiers are always popular. Favored pets in photographs can further enhance collectibility since there is a ready market for photographs with dogs and cats. Amateur views that document home interiors are historically important and valuable. Post mortem portraits are actively collected and those of deceased African Americans are less common than other groups during this period. A collector appraising the value of any photograph needs to ask "What does this photograph say about the black experience?" and its corollary "How could this be used in a book or museum exhibit to illustrate black life from a previous era?"

— One area of opportunity in collecting photography in general is related to the aesthetic or artistic quality of a photograph. Well posed portraits of attractive children and young women remain popular among collectors of all picture formats. A photograph that transcends being a mere recording of someone or some place to being truly art is something that is not recognized by everyone. An identified photographer only increases its value.

— As it has been common with earlier family photo albums, interesting photographs are often removed and groups are broken up in order to maximize a collector's or dealer's return on an investment. The sum of the parts may thought to be worth more than the total. Consequently, totally intact albums are becoming scarcer to find. If you find one that contains a unique and interesting collection of images that have been carefully mounted and identified, avoid the temptation to break it up. Once dispersed, these collections can never be put back together again and the historical context of who, what, when, and where of the photographs is lost forever.

— Some of the highest priced photo postcards can also be the most troubling to view. Since this medium made it easier to document the world outside the photographer's studio, the racism of the era became subject to the camera's eye as well. Photographs that document racial segregation, black lynchings and the human toll of racial violence are part and parcel of images of this era and in demand among collectors.

A view of the railroad station (above) at Southern Pines, North Carolina, documented the "separate but equal" practices of the Jim Crow era. Two anonymous ladies are visible through the window in the "WAITING ROOM FOR COLORED PEOPLE" to the far left of the center room which, as the enlarged detail (below, left) shows, was reserved for whites.

Two "cowboys" recreate a mock hanging for this photo postcard made by Bert Covell in Birmingham, Alabama. The National Association for the Advancement of Colored People reported that 3436 lynchings occurred in the United States from 1889 to 1922.

Focal Point: **The First Black Celebrity Athlete**

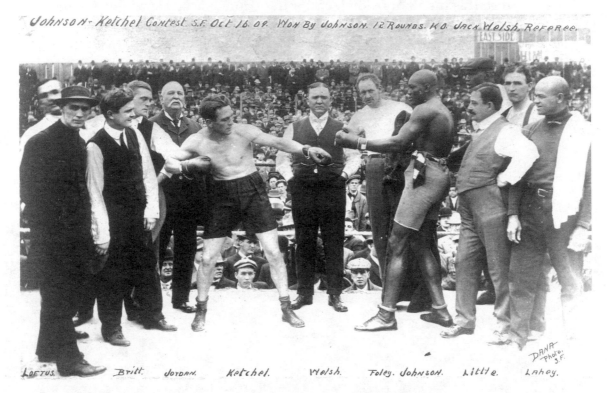

On October 16, 1909, Jack Johnson met Stanley Ketchel in California to defend his heavyweight title. This photograph was made just before the fight began and was later sold as a photo postcard. Johnson won by knocking out Ketchel in the 12th round.

The use of negatives in photography, whether they were made of glass or flexible film, made possible the mass production of inexpensive photographs of famous people. One of the first black athletes in the United States to have his photographs widely circulated was a boxer that many Americans loved to hate — Jack Johnson.

John Arthur "Jack" Johnson was born in Galveston, Texas, on March 31, 1878. Leaving school at an early age, he claimed to have fought his first regular fight when almost sixteen years old. Jack began his boxing career sometimes promoted as "Little Artha." By 1897, he had become a professional boxer having grown to just over six feet tall. Due to the racism of Jim Crow America, he was only allowed at first to fight other black boxers as he toured around the country. After many victories, he won the title of Colored Heavyweight Champion in 1903 when he defeated Denver Ed Martin in a fight that lasted twenty rounds. However, he was not yet allowed to compete for the World Heavyweight title because of his race.

In 1907, Jack fought Bob Fitzsimmons, an ex-heavyweight champion and a white athlete, in Philadelphia and won by knocking out the ex-champ in the second round. Current champions refused to fight Johnson because of his race until an Australian, Tommy Burns, won the heavyweight title. Burns finally agreed to a bout in Sidney, Australia, to prove he was the truly the best heavyweight fighter and the two met in December 1908. After battling for fourteen rounds, the fight was halted by the police and the referee awarded the victory to Johnson. To the shock and dismay of many whites, an African American was now the World Heavyweight Champion for the first time.

Despite his success, many refused to accept Jack Johnson's talent and the search for a "great white hope" to win back the title began. James Jeffries, a popular white ex-heavyweight champion, left retirement to fight Johnson and "save" the title. Johnson successfully defended his title four times before meeting Jeffries on July 4, 1910 in Reno, Nevada. After battling Jeffries for fifteen rounds, Johnson won the match by a knockout. Many were still not ready to accept him as world champion and the search for another "hope" continued.

While champion, Johnson's lifestyle disturbed many white Americans. Living a flamboyant lifestyle that many envied, he was married three times to white women which many viewed as unacceptable during that time. In 1913, he was convicted of violating the Mann Act for which he was fined $1000 and sentenced to imprisonment for one year and one day. Johnson fled the United States and traveled to France, Spain, Cuba, Mexico and South America until he returned to face his jail term in 1920. In 1915, Johnson had lost his championship title in Havana, Cuba, when he was knocked out by Jess Willard — a loss that many believe was intentional. Johnson grew weary from the pressures of being a fugitive and returned to the United States in 1920 to serve his jail sentence where he fought several successful bouts while in prison in Leavenworth, Kansas. After his release, he continued to fight but never again regained his title.

Jack Johnson died in an automobile accident near Raleigh, North Carolina, on June 10, 1946, but his legend continued to live on. He was inducted into the Boxing Hall of Fame in 1954. *The Great While Hope*, a play based on his life, opened on Broadway in 1968 and was made into a movie released in 1970 with James Earl Jones portraying Johnson.

Curved mount stereocard published in 1910 by E.W. Kelly of Jack Johnson, World Boxing Champion sitting in his Chicago home. This rare stereocard was an attempt to present the controversial champion in a manner that was more acceptable to white America.

According to the inscription on the back of this frame, the subject of the large format albumen photograph taken around 1875 was Adelane Purnell. Adelane had been a slave of the Purnell family on Maryland's Eastern Shore until they had granted her freedom. It noted that she always wore a handkerchief around her head and that one of them was used in this frame as a mat for her photograph. Documented black textiles from the 19th century are rare and highly sought after by collectors.

OTHER STYLES AND FORMATS: 1860-1920s

The formats discussed earlier in this book are those you are most likely to encounter when dealing with 19th and early 20th century photographs of or by African Americans. Black images may also appear in several other styles and formats as well.

Other Card Photographs

Cartes de visite and cabinet cards dominated the styles used for producing paper photographs done in photographers' studios until the end of the 1800s. Smaller and larger photographic prints made on albumen photographic paper (and some other paper types that appeared before the end of the century) that were often mounted on different sizes of card stock were also produced. Though better for framing and display, larger photographs were more costly for the photographer to make and consequently were more expensive, sometimes selling for $1.50 or more depending on size and extra treatments. Few portraits of African Americans are found on the larger format card photographs, particularly before the ending of the Civil War and slavery. The few made before that time often picture blacks as servants to a white family. During the war, outdoor views that were taken in the South of slaves in areas recently occupied by the Union Army were produced in large format for sale in the North. After the war's end, portraits of blacks produced in larger formats increase in number, but are still much less common than those of other Americans. The following sizes (of card mounts) were produced during the 19th century and some formats were given special names:

— "Brady Imperials": 20 x 24 in. (also 17 x 14 in.) introduced in 1857

— Imperial Carte-de-visite (Cabinet Card size): 4 ¼ x 6 ½ in.; introduced in mid 1860s

— Victoria card: 3 ¼ x 5 in.

— Promenade card: 3 ¾ x 7 ½ in. introduced in the 1870s

— Boudoir card: 5 x 8 in. introduced in the 1870s

— Imperial card: term used again for both 8 x 13 in. and 2 ¾ x 17 ⅜ in. sizes introduced in the 1870s.

— Album Gallery Card: "Brady's Album Gallery" views were published during the Civil War in two sizes:
    Small: 2 ⁹⁄₁₆ x 4 ¹⁄₁₆ in.
    Large: 4 ½ x 6 in.

— George Barnard's *Photographic Views of Sherman's Campaign* published in 1866: 12 ¾ x 16 in. mount, 11 x 14 in. print

— Alexander Gardner's *Photographic Sketchbook of the Civil War* published in
1866: 12 ½ x 16 ¾ in. mount; 7 x 9 in. print
— Other sizes: 3 x 4 ⅛ in., 4 ⁵⁄₁₆ x 6 ¹⁄₁₆ in., 5 ⅛ x 7 ¼ in., 5 x 8 in., 5 ¼ x 8 ⅞ in.
By 1900, card photographs were still being made in a variety of mount
sizes which had no specific name. Colors for cardstock used for mounts
ranges from light tan, pale green, to dark grey. Research of clothing
styles and photographers may also help to date the photograph.

Most larger prints were produced by direct contact printing from the glass negative so
print sizes vary depending on the size of negative. Paper prints were then trimmed down
and mounted on cardboard. Standardized large format view cameras sold by the E. & H.T.
Anthony Co., a major supplier of photographic supplies and equipment during the 1800s,
made negatives of the following sizes: 6 ½ x 8 ½ inches, 8 x 10 inches, 10 x 12 inches, 11 x
14 inches, 14 x 17 inches, 17 x 20 inches. For an extra fee, prints could be hand colored by
the photographer or a special "colorist" with oils, water colors, India ink or pastels which,
if skillfully done, could produce very realistic results.

Crayon Portraits

The desire for still larger portraits resembling those painted by artists for society's elite
gave rise to a new photographic format after the Civil War that was used to preserve the
faces of many African Americans. Named the "Crayon Portrait," it was produced from an
enlargement made from a glass or flexible film negative on to photographic paper mounted
on a thin canvas, linen, or cardboard base. The light print was then overpainted by the
photographer with crayon (a term used then for chalk-based pastels and charcoal), ink, or
water color to create what may appear to be an actually hand rendered portrait. These
prints were then often framed in gold painted or gilt frames creating a relatively
inexpensive but elegant form of portraiture compared to those painted by skilled
portraitists. Crayon Portraits were most popular from the mid 1880s until the 1920s though
they are occasionally seen from an earlier date .

Celluloid Button Portraits

Another format used for photographs of African Americans was the celluloid photo
button popular from the around 1900 through the 1920s. Celluloid was patented by John
Wesley Hyatt in 1870 and its use to make buttons for political campaigns was launched
with the 1896 presidential election. Soon celluloid was use to encase photographs for
jewelry such as brooches, lockets, rings and larger medallions. To make the buttons,
specially designed machines folded the edges of the celluloid covered photograph and its
metal backing and a metal rim was inserted inside to hold the package tight. For larger
medallions, another metal backing plate was added that usually had an attached wire or
metal piece so the medallion could be stood upright for display. Printed fancy borders and
elaborate backgrounds were often added to frame the photograph, which were sometimes
hand colored as well. Their durability and modest cost made photo buttons a popular
choice for some African Americans. Unfortunately, the metal backing made it difficult to
record the name of the people in the photograph and most subjects are unknown today.
However, the studios that produced them sometimes stamped their names on the back.

*Crayon portrait of a World War I soldier
in frame with convex glass.*

*Photo button of an unidentified
group of children.*

Panorama albumen photograph of U.S. Colored Troops taken in Virginia, ca. 1864. Most so-called "yard long" panorama photographs were made during the early 1900s enabled by the invention of cameras with rotating lenses. Flexible film and gelatin silver paper were used for printing these scenes.

Close-up of soldiers.

Panorama Photographs

Panorama or "yard long" photographs that record a large group or a wide vista were very popular during the early 1900s through the 1920s. Often used to record World War I military units and camps, school and tourist groups, large businesses and even news worthy events, African Americans are sometimes found as subjects as well. The earliest paper examples were produced by piecing together photographs made from several different angles. By 1899, the first panoramic cameras appeared with a rotating lens that exposed a strip of flexible film as it moved. Prints made on gelatin silver paper (see Chapter 9) from the negatives could be mass produced and offered for sale to everyone pictured in a group.

Circular snapshot on a 4 ¼ x 5 ¼ in. cardboard mount made from an early Kodak box camera. Early Kodak photographs of African Americans are uncommon.

Snapshots

In 1888, George Eastman introduced the Kodak No. 1 box camera that placed photography into the hands of the general public and the snapshot was born. The camera took 100 exposures on flexible roll film instead of glass plates and the owner sent the camera back to Kodak to have the film developed and printed and the camera reloaded. With the slogan "You push the button, we do the rest" promoting the sale of this new marvel, by 1889 Kodak processed over 7,500 prints a day sent in by amateurs. These prints are recognizable and collectable today. The paper photographs of the first Kodak models were mounted on cardboard and the shape of the image was round. Later model cameras eventually made a full frame exposure. Circular prints from the first Kodak box cameras are scarce today and those with black subjects are rare, but can be found. Several models of the Folding Pocket Camera that made negatives of various sizes appeared by the early 1900s. The No. 1 Folding Pocket Kodak camera made the 2 ¼ x 3 ¼ in. picture format which was a popular size for snapshots for many years. Photographs from these cameras were printed on gelatin silver print paper.

Care and Preservation

Recommendations made for the care and preservation of previous formats apply to these photographs as well. Paper photographs should be kept in an area with low humidity and moderate temperature. Transparent archival sleeves can be purchased to protect photographs and acid free archival storage boxes should be used for storage. Do not place them in the sun or display in areas of continual bright light. It would be best to make copies for display and keep the originals properly stored. NEVER use transparent tape to fix tears and NEVER laminate or dry mount originals. Many larger photographs may still be in their original frames that have wooden backs. The acidic lignin in the wood causes woodburn which stains paper and makes it become brittle and deteriorate. Original mats may also be acidic. Photographs need to be removed, matted and framed with archivally approved acid free materials. Seek the advice of a professional conservator before taking action. But be aware that some commercial framing shops have no idea how to properly preserve vintage photographs! Seek recommendations for approved framers from professional curators at large museums or historical societies. Be careful if crayon portraits are removed from their frames since the charcoal or pastels used over the photograph can be rubbed off or smeared. Celluloid button photographs appear sturdy, but the celluloid is very susceptible to warping and fracturing when exposed to high temperatures. Rust forming on the metal backing can also be a problem. Panorama photographs often suffer from exposure to moisture that has caused the gelatin surface of the photographic paper to soften and adhere to the cover glass. DO NOT peel this off as you are likely to remove the layers of photographic emulsion from its paper base! Contact the curator of prints and photographs at your state historical society for advice if your photographs need to be conserved.

Large format albumen photograph (8 x 10 in.) of the son of Frederick, Maryland, photographer J. Davis Byerly posed in the studio with the family's gardener. Taken by Byerly after the Civil War, the photograph is actually a more successful portrait of the unidentified laborer than the photographer's son who had moved slightly during the exposure. Photographs like this are highly sought after by collectors.

Tips for Collecting

— Large photographs of African American subjects can have condition problems due to neglect and mishandling. All are important, but those in excellent condition are rarer and their value further enhanced.

— As in all of the other formats for vintage photographs, bigger is better. Large format photographs were more expensive and those with African Americans are particularly uncommon. Crayon portraits are more common than large format albumen prints and will usually not be valued as high unless there is something particularly compelling about the subject matter.

— Large format photographs of slaves are very rare and in demand. However, there should be strong evidence to support that the subjects were slaves. Outdoor views of slaves are rare and important as well. Those taken during the Civil War that have been widely published are very desirable. Any unpublished views can command an extra premium.

— Unusual subject matter is very desirable. Photographs in all formats picturing black soldiers, sailors, firemen, musicians, sports figures, entertainers and famous individuals are valuable. Panorama photographs of Negro League teams command very high prices. Those of segregated military units are also very collectable.

— Any photographs by African American photographers are very desirable, especially if they recorded other black Americans.

A large format albumen photograph taken by A. Turner, Washington, D.C. recorded Matthew Taylor and his family at his home in Anacostia, Virginia, around 1900. At a time when many photographers usually focused on the primitive cabins and former slave huts of African Americans, this rare portrait documented a black family that had apparently realized the American dream.

Focal Point: A Life Lost and Found

Photograph of Julien Harmon Wilson taken for his 1920 graduation from Ohio State University.

The portrait illustrated above of an African American was purchased from an antique dealer and serves as another link to a previously lost story of triumph and tragedy. The framed photograph is a sepia toned gelatin silver print of distinguished young man inserted into a cardboard folder typical of studio photographs during the first decades of the 20th century. The mount bears the imprint of the Baker Art Gallery in Columbus, Ohio, and has a handwritten inscription that is the key to unraveling its story. The photograph was presented in 1920 to a person whose name cannot be read by J. Harmon Wilson, a student at Ohio State University, in appreciation for having "made this graduation possible." Considering the small number of blacks attending colleges at that time, this was a story that had to be found, and its recovery serves as a guide for researching identified photographs.

Most colleges retain the records of all students that had attended in their history and Ohio State University is no exception. For a small fee, the University Archives was able to supply copies of information that they had available on Julien Harmon Wilson. This included his entries in the *University Directory* for years 1916-1922, commencement programs where he received his Bachelor of Science (1920) and Doctor of Medicine (1922) degrees, and pages from the school yearbook with this photographs. Julien Wilson had become a physician. All colleges and universities attempt to maintain information on graduates as well, and contacting Ohio State's Alumni/Development Information Services produced a wealth of information about Dr. Wilson. Included was his address after graduation, his date and place of birth, the names of his father and mother, his religious denomination, and the name of his wife along with his date of marriage. Also listed was the name of his high school, degrees awarded by the college, and fraternity affiliation which included his membership in prestigious Phi Beta Kappa. The record also noted his service in the Army Medical Corp in World War I.

Armed with Dr. Wilson's first name, it was possible to uncover even more information about him. Turning to the internet to conduct a census search (www.ancestry.com) was not initially successful. Trying various spellings may help, and, in this case, Wilson was found in the 1930 census (the only one in which he appears) with the spelling of "Julian" instead of the correct "Julien." By this time, he had established his practice as a physician and surgeon in Columbus, Ohio. The census also noted that both his mother and father had been born in Georgia which increased the likelihood that Dr. Wilson was the descendant of slaves. A search of the censuses for his parents was inconclusive. The most critical records for locating them were taken in 1890, just two years before Julien's birth, but most of that census was destroyed in a fire and the stories of millions of Americans, including Julien's parents, were lost forever.

Having served in the army during the World War I, Dr. Wilson also had a military record. Service records for over 263,000 soldiers that served during this war from Ohio are also online in searchable database in *Ohio Military Men, 1917-1918* (www.ancestry.com). Here we find that Julien's college career was disrupted when he enlisted and was assigned in July 1918 to the Student's Army Training Corps, Medical Section, at the University of Illinois. Though honorably discharged as private in December 1918, he was recalled to active duty in November 1918 and later discharged in 1922 after promotion to the rank of first lieutenant. During this service, he was able to complete the requirements needed to earn his medical degree. Though he never served overseas during the war, he went to France for a year in 1922 as an exchange scholar at the University of Lyons and completed an internship there.

After his return, Dr. Wilson established his practice in Columbus, Ohio, where he was successful enough to be noted in *Who's Who in Colored America, 1933-37*.

Unfortunately, this outstanding career came to a tragic end. Typed on his alumni record was a notation added in 1941 that Dr. Julien Harmon Wilson had died on May 25 of that year in an auto accident, and the life of man who had realized the dream of his ancestors was lost. Undoubtedly, additional investigation will uncover even more of this story which is part of the challenge and fun of researching old photographs and rediscovering people from the past.

Ohio photography studio around the time Julien Wilson sat for his graduation portrait in 1920. Note the addition of an electric light (left) to supplement the skylight.

In this gelatin silver print taken during the 1950s, an unidentified photographer uses a large format camera to make a photograph of a wedding party posed inside his studio. By this time, electric lights had totally replaced the skylight found in early galleries.

GELATIN SILVER PRINTS

During the 1880s, a new photographic paper emerged that was used to make the greatest number of photographs of African Americans than all of the earlier processes combined. The use of albumen photographic paper during this period began to be replaced by commercially manufactured collodion and gelatin printing out papers. ("Printing out" paper did not need to be chemically developed to produce a positive image from a negative.) Gelatin "developing out" paper, which had to be submerged in a developing solution to make the photograph appear on the paper, soon followed and eventually became the dominant type of photographic paper used from around 1905 to the present.

Gelatin developing out paper had several layers. The base was the paper which came in many different sizes and weight or thickness. A opaque white coating was applied over the paper (technically the baryta layer) on one side. The paper was then coated with a transparent gelatin binder emulsion that contained the light-sensitive silver salts. In this layer, the photographic image was formed. Using an enlarger, light (now from an electric light bulb) was projected through a flexible film negative and a lens to expose the photographic paper. The use of an enlarging lens made it possible to make large prints from a small negative that no longer had to be directly contact printed to get bold, detailed images. After dipping the exposed paper in a developer (which caused the image to appear) and a fixer bath (which made the paper light insensitive), the familiar black-and-white print appeared. Gelatin papers were produced in many types of surface textures along with glossy (shiny) and matte (flat) finishes. This photographic paper was adopted by amateur and professional photographers after 1905 as well as photo finishing businesses that offered film development and printing services. By the 1920s, nearly all photographs were being produced this way due to its low cost and fast production time. Photographs made on this gelatin printing out paper are more commonly known today as gelatin silver prints or simply black-and-white prints. Unlike earlier paper photographs, these were not usually mounted on cardboard after the early 1900s. They are usually found slipped into cardboard sleeves, glued into snapshot albums, or loose.

Care and Preservation

The greatest enemy of gelatin silver prints is heat and humidity. Heat will cause the emulsion to soften and stick to surfaces with which it comes into contact such as the cover glass of a frame. Once adhered, it is very difficult if not impossible to remove without damaging the print. The photograph can even stick to the surface of transparent archival sleeves as well. Due to different rates of expansion and contraction of the photograph's different layers, exposure to high humidity will also cause the prints to curl from the edges inward. This may cause the emulsion to fracture. Storage in low humidity (30-50%) and moderate temperature (less than

This snapshot was made from a Folding Pocket Kodak camera like the one seen in this 2 ¼ x 3 ¼ in. photograph. Over the years, the gelatin silver print has been scratched and soiled from neglect. Conservation should only be undertaken by a skilled professional.

65°) is ideal, but a comfortable and stable environment as close as possible to these standards will help preserve them. Never store these prints in attics or basements where they may be exposed to extremes in temperature and humidity. Avoid exposure to direct sunlight and fluorescent bulbs which emit large amounts of ultraviolet radiation that can cause photographs to fade. Plastic UV filters that fit around these bulbs can be purchased to protect prints (see "Additional Resources"). If negatives are still present, they can be stored in transparent archival sleeves for organizing and handling. Do not attempt to clean or repair original prints. NEVER repair tears with transparent tape. Copies can be made of original prints with a digital camera or scanner and computer programs used to restore an image.   Digital prints then can be made for display or sharing with family and friends. When writing identifications on the back of gelatin silver prints (or any earlier paper format photographs), use a soft lead pencil since ink from a pen may bleed through and damage the image on the front. Be sure to include the names of people in the photograph, where and when it was taken, what was occurring and don't forget the name of the photographer! Consult with the curator of photographs and prints at your state historical society for further advice for care and conservation of originals.

Tips for Collecting

Gelatin silver prints were used to produce amateur snapshots, formal studio portraits, artistic, commercial and news photographs, as well as to record other important moments of life. From the snapshots and studio portraits of the newborn baby, to the annual school and class pictures, graduations, wedding portraits and reception photographs, birthday parties, holiday moments, new cars, vacation shots and even funerals, the lives of African Americans as well as others were recorded for posterity in a quantity that had been previously unavailable. The following tips will help you to evaluate the collectibility and value of these photographs.

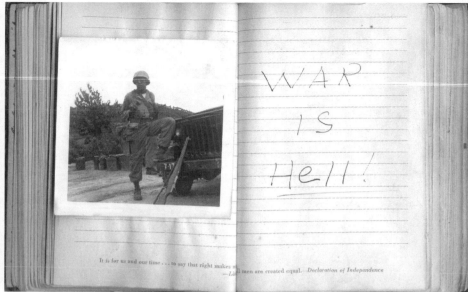

In his diary My Life in the Army *(left), an African American soldier during World War II, identified only by his army serial number, recorded his candid opinions about army life, the war, and his many friends while serving on New Guinea and the Philippine Islands. His name was discovered by searching the free online "World War II Army Serial Number Merged File" on the website of the National Archives (www.nara.gov). Photograph albums and diaries kept by black soldiers are scarce and very collectible.*

— As is the case with earlier photographic formats, photographs may suffer condition problems due to improper storage and neglect. Since the original negatives have often been lost, these prints can still have importance and value. Digital restoration of photographs today can work wonders in rescuing images from the past.

— Photographs by black photographers are in demand. An established market already exists for the work of James VanDerZee, Cornelius Battey, Addison Skurlock, and Gordon Parks, but others await discovery.

— Newspaper and wire service photographs of important African Americans and events are in demand. The invention of the half-tone process made it possible for newspapers to begin adding photographs by the 1880s. The photograph archives of newspapers that have gone out of business in recent years can contain important images that document the African American experience.

— Sports photographs of black athletes are in demand, especially relating to the Negro League teams in baseball. Autographed material will also add an additional premium.

— Albums with mounted photographs, especially ones that include captions, are desirable. Those assembled by World War I and World War II soldiers are uncommon and in demand among collectors. Personal snapshot albums are also sought after, especially if the subject matter is interesting and the photographs well composed.

Olympic champion Jesse Owens distributed this photograph when making personal appearances around the country. He signed this for a student who had invited Jesse to speak at a high school.

These gelatin silver prints are part of an album that belonged to Moses Dixon. The pose of the unidentified soldier (left) taken in France in 1944 is similar to that of his ancestors during the Civil War. Dixon also had his photograph (right) taken in France. Before World War II, he was a member of Company 2317 of the Civilian Conservation Corps at Beltsville, Maryland (bottom).

— Photographs that document both discrimination and the Civil Rights protest movement are extremely important. Images of the activists, leaders, organizations, and protests document a major chapter in American history that demands their preservation.

— Promotional photographs for black entertainers are in demand, especially for early jazz and blues performers. Those that are autographed can command an additional premium. Promotional "stills" for advertising black movies are also collected.

— Beware of nitrate negatives! These may be marked with the word "nitrate" by the manufacturer on the edge of the film. As it decomposes, nitrate film gives off hazardous fumes and can burst into fire if stored improperly. Read National Park Service Conserve-O-Gram 14/9 "Identification of Film-Base Photographic Materials" (see "Additional Resources") and seek the advice of a museum professional for help!

— Beware of reproductions! Prints from the original negatives that were made close to the time that the photograph was taken, especially if they were made by the original photographer, will always command higher prices from collectors than much later printings from original or copy negatives. It is easy to re-photograph an original vintage print and reproduce it on gelatin developing out paper. Think of this like a book — first printings of first editions are always more desirable among collectors than later printings/ editions. If you are not sure, get a written guarantee from the seller that includes a complete description of the photograph and the time period that the print you are purchasing was made. Also remember that even if a photograph is a vintage printing, many copies may have been made which can affect the value.

Gelatin silver print of Martin Luther King, Jr. taken in January 1964.

BILLIE HOLIDAY

Personal Management
JOE GLASER
R C A Building 30 Rockefeller Plaza
New York N. Y.

Original gelatin silver prints of black entertainers can be very collectible. Photographs of singer Billie Holiday (left) were distributed to promote her concerts and record albums. A picture taken for the newspapers recorded opera singer Marian Anderson (right) singing at the Lincoln Memorial on Easter Sunday in 1939 after she was denied the right to sing at Constitution Hall in Washington, D.C. Cab Calloway (below), a pioneer of modern popular music, used gelatin silver prints to promote his band as well.

Focal Point: **Moorer of Philadelphia**

Moorer was a professional photographer with a keen eye who worked from the 1920s to the 1960s in Philadelphia. He is an example of African Americans whose work can still be discovered.

These gelatin silver prints (above) and on the following pages are just a very small sampling of the remarkable work by black photographer Moorer. A group of boys were recorded celebrating Christmas (left). Shoe repairman John Alexander (right) was described in Moorer's album as "A Kindly Old Gentleman (Deceased)."

Receiving instruction.

A Philadelphia fraternity.

As an aspiring amateur and later as a professional, Moorer always recorded his Philadelphia community with dignity and respect.

The Post Office.

An auto repair shop.

An unidentified lady.

The bride to be.

Moorer's photographs exhibit his talents at composition and posing and the photographer's ability to coax engaging expressions from many of his subjects.

The birthday party.

Based on the style of dress and card mount, this cabinet card of an unidentified black girl looks to have been taken during the 1890s. Checking the author's Directory of Maryland Photographers, 1839-1900 *finds that the Darby Studio was in business at this location only from 1900-01 and adds a more specific date for when it was made.*

10

GUIDE TO RESEARCHING AFRICAN AMERICAN SOLDIERS & CIVILIANS

The Civil War

During the Civil War, 178,975 African Americans served in the Union Army and 9,596 served in the U.S. Navy.   Occasionally, photographs of these men are found that have a name and no other information written on it by the subject or someone who received the momento. This is most commonly found on cartes de visite since the cardboard mount was easier to write on, though ambrotypes and tintypes can carry identifications which are sometimes written inside the miniature case. Several resources can be used to find out about the subject of the portrait depending upon how much initial information the inscription provides. The following can help you uncover the story of the soldier in your photograph.

Step One: The Civil War Soldiers and Sailors System

To learn more about the person in your photograph, the first step is to find out the name of the military unit he served with if it was not already found with the photograph. Today it is very easy and free to access this information thanks to the tireless efforts of citizen volunteers. Soon after the Civil War, a huge project was conducted to officially record every person who fought for the Union. Every government document was read and an individual file with a master index card was created for every name mentioned which included the person's name, unit of service and rank. The information from every index card has been entered into a computer data base known as **The Civil War Soldiers and Sailors System.** This online system is maintained by the National Park Service that will eventually include 5.4 million names of Americans both North and South who served in their respective armies and navies during the Civil War. It was first launched in 1996 with the names of 235,000 (some are listed in more than one unit) African American Union soldiers. To find out more about your soldier or sailor,

1. Access the internet and direct your browser to: **www.civilwar.nps.gov**

2. Click on "Soldiers" or "Sailors" to go to the searchable database link.

3. Enter in the first and last name of the individual and any other information about him that is requested and then click on "Submit Inquiry." For sailors, click on "Search."

4. For soldiers, a window will come up with his name and the name of his regiment. Clicking on his name will give some more detail of what was on the index card. Clicking on the regiment's name will take you to a summary of that unit's action during the war. For sailors, a window will appear with the person's Name, Age, Complexion (Negro or Mulatto) Occupation, and Home. Clicking on the name again will take you to a more

detailed record of their personal information and their service including Height, Dates of Enlistment, Rating (rank), and the Detailed Muster Record that lists the names of ships served on and the dates the sailor was recorded.

> **Note**: If your image only contains a name, your research may be more complicated. A common name, such as John Johnson, produces 2105 rows of individual records! To find the right man, you can limit your search to only "Colored" units and use any additional information you gain from studying the actual photograph. This includes determining, if possible, their branch of service (infantry, cavalry, artillery, etc.), approximate age, rank, distinctive uniform style that indicates a particular state or unit, or additional dating attributes (inscriptions, format of photograph, presence of tax stamps, years of photographer's activity at a specific location). The location of an identified photographer's studio can also be a clue to the soldier's home state.

Explore the site to see if any of the other databases are also helpful. More information will added in the future making this site a valuable research tool.

Other Online Resources: The Civil War and Genealogy Data Base

Another online option is the Civil War and Genealogy Database website on the internet (**www.civilwardata.com**). For a fee, this site provides a searchable database similar to that of the National Park Service. However, its records can include more detailed information about a soldier that is not found on the free NPS site.

Upon arrival on the homepage, you can purchase a $10 Visitor Pass that is good for 7 day site access to the genealogy database. This pass allows you to examine only individual military records of officers and enlisted men. Unlimited access for one year costs $25 which gives access to all of the site's databases. Once you subscribe to either membership level, conducting a name search will give you access to more complete information that includes the units in which the man served, all ranks achieved and dates of promotions, and how the individuals service was terminated. Summaries of regimental action are available through the Annual Subscription that can help expand the information about this soldier's service. A searchable database of identified photographs is also included through the expanded membership that may put a face with the name you are researching. **Note:** This database is also available for a fee though **www.ancestry.com** which also includes access to other useful records including the **Civil War Pension Index.** This searchable database provides links to view the actual index card for the Union soldier which includes the names of dependents, the names of all military units in which he served, and pension file number which you can use if you order copies of these records from the National Archives.

Step Two: The National Archives Research

The most complete documentation of a Civil War soldier's service is going to be found among the military service records at the National Archives and Records Administration in Washington, D.C. Records can be obtained by mail and in person. A Union soldier's record will include both his Compiled Military Service File accumulated during this actual service and his pension file if he survived the war and applied for a later pension or if his widow or dependents applied for his pension.

Research by Mail: Once you know the individual's name and unit, you have two ways to obtain copies of these records. To get the Compiled Military Service File of an individual soldier, you can either order them online or submit **NATF Form 86**. Cost is $17.00. For copies of the complete pension file, you can order it online or through the mail by submitting **NATF Form 85**. The fee is $37.00. You can now use a credit card to order copies of these files online. Go to the National Archive website (listed below) and click on the "Research Room" link to see how. You will need to know at least the soldiers first and last name, branch of service (Army, Marines, Navy), and the name of the state from which he served. Information found on the previously mentioned websites will help archivists find your person. Copies of Forms 85 and 86 currently cannot be downloaded from the National Archives, but they can be ordered by filling out an online order form or sending a letter to the:

> **National Archives and Records Administration,**
> **Attn: NWCTB,**
> **700 Pennsylvania Ave.,**
> **Washington, D.C. 20408-00001**.

Be sure to provide your name and postal mailing address, the specific form number, and the number of forms needed (limit of 5). For more information, visit the National Archives and Records Administration website (**www.nara.gov**).

On Site Research: The complete records for a Civil War soldiers can also be accessed by a visit to the National Archives and Records Administration building in Washington, D.C. Enter on the business side (700 Pennsylvania Ave.) which is on the opposite side of the building where tourists enter to see the Declaration of Independence and U.S. Constitution on Constitution Ave. Once you pass through security, proceed to the Microform Reading Room on the first floor. There, you will sign in and be assigned a microfilm viewing machine.

> **Note:** Eventually, you will need to use the Central Research Room on the third floor of the Washington, D.C. building and this requires a "Researcher Identification Card" that allows you to enter. You will need some form of identification that includes your photo and will be instructed to fill out a short form that describes your research project. Ask the guards at the entrance for directions about obtaining this card which is good for one year. A Researchers Identification Card is **not** needed when only using the Microform Reading Room.

It will have helped to have identified the unit in which your Union Civil War soldier served if you had not already done so online (see **Step One**). If you do not know it, you might still find this information through several resources. First check the microfilm rolls of the "Index to Compiled Service Records of Volunteer Union Soldiers Who Served with United States Colored Troops" **(Record Group 94, M589)**. This is an alphabetical listing of the index cards to the compiled service records of the U.S. Colored Troops which will include the information found online in Step One. If your soldier survived the war and applied for a pension or had a dependent apply for a pension, check the *General Index to Pension Files, 1861-1934*, **T288** (part of Record Group 15, 49, 217). This is a general index to the pension files and is arranged alphabetically showing a card that contains the name of the veteran; name and class of dependent, if any; the service unit; the application, file, and certificate number; and the state from which the claim was filed.

Once you know the soldier's unit, complete **NATF Form 86** to request to see the actual military service records and **NATF Form 85** for the pension file. These forms can be obtained both in the Microform Reading Room and the Central Research Room. Once completed, submit these to the information desks. It takes several hours for the files to be retrieved so ask the information personnel if there is enough time to see the files on the day of your visit. (**Note:** if you already know the name and unit of your soldier, you can call a few days ahead of time to have the files pulled so they are ready on the designated day of your visit.) Files will be viewed in the Central Research Room (3rd floor) where you will need the Researcher's Identification Card to enter. Photo copier machines are available.

Researching African American Soldiers: 1866-1916

At the end of the Civil War, the United States government reorganized the military to meet the needs of the Reconstruction era. By Act of Congress of July 28, 1866, two new regiments of colored cavalry troops (9th and 10th U.S. Cavalry) and four colored infantry regiments (38th, 39th, 40th, 41st) were created marking the first time black troops had been incorporated into the Regular Army. Later in March 1869, the army was further restructured. The colored cavalry troops remained the same, but the four infantry regiments were consolidated into the 24th U.S. Infantry (from the old 38th and 41st regiments) and the 25th U.S. Infantry (from the old 39th and 40th regiments). These cavalry and infantry regiments went on to distinguished duty as "Buffalo Soldiers" out west, but researching them is more time consuming because the information is currently not available in any searchable electronic databases.

To start your research, you will need to know which of the regiments your soldier served with if he was in the service before 1898. This information can be found in two ways. The first way is to go the Main Research Room (you need to have a Researcher Card) at the National Archives to search the Regular Army Enlistment Papers, 1798-1894 (**Record Group 94, Records of the Adjutant General's Office, 1780s-1917, entry 91**). In this record group, the records for all enlistments in the Regular Army during this period are presented alphabetically. These records include their name, place of enlistment, date, name of enlistment officer, age, occupation, personal description, regimental assignment, and certification of the examining surgeon and recruiting officer. An alternative approach can be taken by searching the microfilm rolls (**M233**) of the Registers of Enlistment in the United States Army, 1798-1914 (**Record Groups 94, 391, and 407**). These records can also be accessed in the Microform Reading Room at the National Archives. The enlistment records may include the individual's name; when, where and by whom he was enlisted; period of enlistment; place of birth; age at time of enlistment; civilian occupation; physical description; unit or regiment to which he was assigned; and additional remarks. Records are organized by groups of years and then alphabetically by surname (last name). It may be necessary to search the records of several year categories to find your man.

If the soldier served from 1898-1902 in regular military units or state and federal volunteer units during the Spanish-American War or the Philippine Insurrection, your research is now easier. (Congress created two black volunteer units in 1899, the 48th and 49th Infantry Regiments, to serve along with the four colored regular infantry and cavalry regiments.) You can order his Compiled Military Service File and Federal Military

Pension File online or through the mail using **NATF Form 86** and his pension file (if he qualified for one) using **NATF Form 85** as described in the guide to researching Civil War records. The cost is the same as that charged for the Civil War records.

Several other record groups at the National Archives can provide even more about your soldier. Though time consuming to search, the information found may not be available anywhere else.

Within the "Returns From Regular Army Infantry Regiments, June 1821-December 1916" **(M665)**, microfilm rolls 245-253 contain copies of the returns for the 24th Infantry organized yearly from Dec. 1866-Dec. 1916. Microfilm rolls 254-261 contain copies of the returns for the 25th Infantry organized by year from Jan 1867-Dec. 1916. Be sure to start with the 1869 returns on each of the first rolls since that marks the beginning of the records for the colored regiment. In these records, the unit strength and total number of men present, absent, sick, or on extra daily duty along with officers and enlisted men listed by name will be found. The station of the unit and a record of events as well as other information that was periodically required was also included. Within the "Returns from Regular Cavalry Regiments, 1833-1916" **(M744)** are found the records for the 9th and 10th Cavalry. Microfilm rolls 87-94 cover the 9th Cavalry from Oct. 1866-Dec. 1916 and rolls 95-102 cover from Sept. 1866-Dec. 1916 for the 10th Cavalry. Even more detailed information can be found with the monthly "Post Returns" submitted by the commander of an army post. Within the huge file (1550 rolls of microfilm) of the "Returns From United States Military Posts, 1800-1916" **(M617),** the records of an individual U.S. Army post anywhere in the world can be searched for a specific time period.

In addition, 54 African American soldiers and sailors received the Medal of Honor from the Civil War through the Spanish-American War. Their stories will be found in the microfilm rolls **(M929)** for "Documents Relating to the Military and Naval Service of Blacks Awarded the Congressional Medal of Honor from the Civil War to the Spanish-American War."

Service records for World War I and later are stored at the National Personnel Records Center in St. Louis, Missouri. Unfortunately, many of these records were destroyed by a fire in 1972. Copies of records can be ordered through the mail by a veteran or immediate family (next-of-kin) of a deceased veteran by mail. The general public can also order copies of files, but the information provided can be restricted. Information that can be provided to researchers includes name, service number, rank, dates of service, awards and decorations, place of entrance and separation. If the veteran is deceased, his place of birth, date and geographical location of death and place of burial can also be provided. Visit the website of the National Archives (**www.nara.gov**) for more information.

Researching African American Civilians

Sometimes early photographs are found with names and there may be a desire to learn more about these individuals. A complete discussion of all of the resources that flesh out the life of someone captured in a photograph could be one or more books in itself. There are, however, some basic sources of information that might shed some light on your subjects, a few of which are freely available on the internet and others that charge a fee for access.

Starting Your Search

After collecting as much information as possible from family members and records, the next step for genealogical research is usually the U.S. Census. Taken every ten years since 1790, the records covering up to 1930 are open to the public for research (records are closed for 72 years after they are taken to protect privacy). These census records are on microfilm and available at many public libraries, college and university libraries, state archives, and historical societies as well as the National Archives in Washington, D.C. and its regional centers around the country (check **www.nara.gov** to find these locations). The censuses are indexed and the census entries for specific individuals can often be located quickly once you become familiar with working with these records. They are also available on the internet, though fees may be charged for access.

Using the Internet

Several websites provide online access to all of the census records currently open to the public as well as many other searchable databases. Among these is Ancestry.com (**www.ancestry.com**) that advertises "the largest collection of family history records on the Web." Cost for access to their information depends on the databases that you wish to access and whether you want a monthly or an annual subscription. All of the census records are indexed and searchable by names. The complete information for individual that is found in the record is provided as well as links to view the actual census pages that bear their names. It should be noted that it was not until the 1850 census that the name of every family member or other free persons living at a specific location were listed. Before that, only the head of household was identified. Also be aware that most of the 1890 census was destroyed in a fire and only a very limited number of records survived. This website also has many other databases available including the Civil War Pension Index that can used to order copies of the files online from the National Archives (**www.nara.gov**).

Other research sites offer census access as well that can be found through an internet search. Free access to online records that could be helpful are at the website of The Church of Jesus Christ of Latter-Day Saints (**www.familysearch.org**). Here you can conduct free searches of the 1880 U.S. Census and the U.S. Social Security Death Index. The public information in these records will be provided to you online. Many public libraries also offer free online access to genealogy research sites. Check with your local library to see what is available.

Slavery Research

The biggest challenge for doing African American genealogical research is the issue of slavery. The small portion of the black population not held in bondage was initially recorded as "All Other Free People" (1790, 1800, 1810) or as "Free Colored Persons" (1820, 1830, 1840). The censuses of 1850 and 1860 recorded each individual's "Color" as white, black, or mulatto. Only the heads of free African American families were recorded until 1850 when the names of all family members were added from that point on. Those held in bondage were just recorded as a total number (1790, 1800, 1810) or by sex which was then broken down into general age categories (1820, 1830, 1840). In 1850 and 1860, a separate Slave Schedule was taken as part of the census that gives the name of the owner, the sex, color, and ages of each individual slave. Names of slaveholders in these census records can be searched online at Ancestry.com (**www.ancestry.com**). Unfortunately, none of the names of slaves were recorded. The use of other records and family tradition may help to place a name with these impersonal descriptions. Also check the free databases at AfriGeneas (**www.afrigeneas.com**) where names of slaves and their owners are being collected.

Other Records

After slavery was abolished, search for African American families as well as others becomes easier. All members of a family along with other residents at a location are individually listed in the censuses with an increasing amount of personal information about each individual as time goes on. Indexes to the censuses make it easier to find an individual in America's rapidly expanding population. Other resources, such as city directories which can date from as early as the late 1790s (similar to phone books of today) can help locate people along with their residence and occupation during the years between the censuses. Many of these for local areas are available on microfilm today at public libraries, state archives, colleges, and historical societies. The Library of Congress in Washington, D.C. also has a national collection of city directories. Many state archives are also now making these directories available online for free. Fee based sites offer them too. The Maryland State Archives (**www.mdarchives.state.md.us**) has Baltimore City directories from 1827-1858/59, Annapolis city directories (1910, 1924), as well as the Coleman *Colored Directories of Professional, Clerical, Skilled and Business Directories* from 1913 to 1945/46 online. Use an internet search engine to see what might be available. Directories of photography studios (see "Additional Resources") may also help determine a time period for your photograph. More specific information on conducting genealogical research can be found in numerous guide books. Research takes some effort and persistence, but the discoveries that you can make about the photographs of family members and others can be very rewarding.

Professional research services are available to search military and civilian records for a fee. Visit www.HistoricGraphics.com for more information.

This albumen photograph of William Henry Demby, 4th United States Colored Infantry, is a photographic enlargement copied sometime during or soon after the Civil War from his wartime carte de visite. The photograph was then painted over by the photographer or colorist which gives it the appearance of being an original oil painting. Courtesy of Gil Barrett.

Focal Point: **Researching a Civil War Soldier**

The stories of the almost 180,000 African Americans who served in the United States Colored Troops during the Civil War continue to be uncovered as researchers try to fill in these previously unwritten pages of American history. The lives of these men recorded in photographs, particularly if the subject is identified, present an exciting opportunity for discovery when the tools of modern research are properly used. Uncovering the story of Corporal William Demby, 4th U. S. Colored Infantry, serves as a compelling model for conducting the research of Civil War soldiers.

The photograph and the promotion certificate of Corporal Demby appeared together in mail/phone auction and were illustrated in the sale's catalogue. The picture was described as a painting, but it turned out to actually be a painted albumen photograph when it was obtained by the successful bidder. (For an extra fee photographs could be hand tinted by photographers or their "colorists" and these are sometimes mistaken for paintings.) The accompanying certificate, which was a rare addition, documented the promotion of Demby to the rank of corporal in January 1864. No other research on the soldier was offered.

Uncovering the service experience of Corporal Demby began with checking the various internet databases already discussed in this book. A search of the National Park Service's free Civil War Soldiers & Sailors System (**www.civilwar.nps.gov**) found nine soldiers named "William Demby" — three of whom served with the 4th U.S. Colored Infantry! Fortunately, only one had "H." as a middle initial (which was given on his promotion certificate) and held the rank of corporal. Checking his entry confirmed Demby's enrollment as corporal in Co. G, 4th U.S. Colored Infantry and stated that his name was on a plaque at the African American Civil War Memorial at 10th Street and Vermont Avenue in Washington, D.C. Going next to the fee-based genealogy website Ancestry.com (**www.ancestry.com**) added more pieces to reconstructing William's life. The site's American Civil War Soldiers database recorded his enlistment in the 4th U.S. Colored Infantry on August 11, 1863 and provided some surprising information. Under his Service Record, it was noted that he had been wounded and that he died from his wounds on March 3, 1865 — just a little more than a month before the end of the Civil War. No other details about his death were given and a more extensive investigation into the life and death of this soldier, who had made the ultimate sacrifice for his country, was now even more important. The search now turned to the National Archives.

The details of Corporal Demby's as well as other Union soldiers from the Civil War is found in their compiled service records. These records are found at the Washington, D.C. branch of the National Archives where either the original or microfilmed file can be accessed and copies can be made there or ordered by mail. The Compiled Service Records of the 4th U.S. Colored Infantry have been microfilmed and were available in the Microform Reading Room. William H. Demby's record was found on Roll 35. There was recorded William's physical description that had been transcribed from the Descriptive Book for Company G (physical descriptions, but no photographs, were kept to identify soldiers in case of death or desertion). Demby was described as being 19 years old when he enlisted, 5 ft. 6 in. tall, brown complexion, black eyes and having black hair. He was born in Queen Anne County on Maryland's Eastern Shore and had the occupation as a farmer before his enlistment. It also confirmed his death on March 3, 1865 from wounds received in action. Entries from his company's muster rolls recorded that he had enlisted for 3 years

William Demby received this certificate when he was promoted to the rank of corporal on August 26, 1864. This type of document is rarely found accompanying photographs of African American soldiers.

along with the dates he was present for duty. From the July/August 1864 entry, we learn that William was "free before April 19, 1861" and that he was not a slave at the beginning of the Civil War. This information was recorded because of the discrimination over pay for black soldiers who received $10 a month instead of the $13 paid to white soldiers. In July 1864, Congress acted to end this practice by authorizing equal pay, retroactive to January 1, 1864, for all who had been free as of April 19, 1861. William qualified for the pay raise and his back pay. Shortly thereafter, the records noted that he had been wounded in action on September 29, 1864. This proved to not be fatal since he returned to duty the following month. Unfortunately, this was not the case about five months later when his records state that he died March 3, 1865 "by reason of wounds received in action." Additional entries document that he was wounded in the left leg on February 11, 1865 near Fort Fisher, North Carolina, in the Battle of Sugar Loaf. Having broken the bones, his leg was amputated and he was put on the transport ship *S.R. Spaulding* where he died on March 3, 1865. His body was taken to an army hospital in Baltimore before his remains were sent home to Queen Anne County. Though he had no personal property at the time of his death, it was noted that he still owed the regimental sutler $10.00. William was one of 1,102 enlisted men of the U.S. Colored Troops who died of wounds received in action during the Civil War.

The Pension Files are an important resource for information about Civil War soldiers, even those who did not survive the war, and they are always worth checking. The Index to the Pension File can be searched online (**www.ancestry.com**) and on microfilm at the National Archives. Copies of files can be ordered by mail (**www.nara.gov**). Though he died during the war, these records provided a great deal of information about the lives of William H. Demby and his family. Men who had served in the Union army during the war as well as their widows, orphans and the parents of soldiers who had depended on their

A card (left) from Demby's service file documents his death in March 1865 and that he was owed back pay. His mother's 1867 pension application (right) was found in the Civil War Pension Files.

sons for financial support could receive a federal pension. William's mother, Hester Bedford, applied in June 1867 on the grounds that her son had been her sole means of income. In the records of her case, we learn that Hester had been born free and that William's father, whose last name William bore, was a slave who had never married William's mother. He died in 1846 and Hester married John Bedford who was also a slave of a Mr. Tilghman. Bedford, who died in 1862, provided little if any financial support for his wife so it was necessary for Hester to hire out her son, her only child, to work as a farmer to support her until his enlistment in the army. Once in the service, the mother claimed that her son, who had not married or had any children, sent home much of his pay for her support and she offered the sworn testimony of friends to verify her claim. As additional evidence, the file contained a letter that William had written to her in which he mentioned that he included some of his pay. This was particularly interesting since his mother was apparently illiterate and could only make her mark when signing her name to all of these official documents.

Finally, after twenty-four years had passed since Hester Bedford's initial 1867 application, she was granted a pension in 1891 for her son's service. Her case was initially dropped under her first attorneys, but another lawyer took up her cause in 1888. Hester received $8.00 a month going back to March 3, 1865 which increased to $12.00 monthly on March 19, 1886. The money must have provided at least some comfort during her final days having lost her only child in the war. Hester Bedford died on August 13, 1899 having received her last pension check on June 4. Her grave and that of her son, William, still remain to be discovered. William H. Demby's photograph and promotion certificate remain a testament to one man's sacrifice for his country and his face is one of the few that can be connected to the thousands of names of United States Colored Troops on the tablets of the African American Civil War Memorial.

11

ADDITIONAL RESOURCES

The first automated photo booths were introduced by the International Mutoscope Reel Co., Inc. in the 1930s and became popular in arcades and train stations through the 1950s. The booths made a gelatin silver print that was enclosed in a 2 x 3 inch metal frame. Since these inexpensive photographs were made for several decades, clothing styles and the age of identified subjects can help to date them.

Other Photograph Dating Clues

The following technological advances in photography may also provide you with some clues for dating photographs taken during the 1900s.

1902 – Kodak introduced "Velox" photographic paper for making black-and-white prints. It was often used for snapshots remained in use through the 1950s. The paper has its name printed on the reverse.

1934 – Kodak introduced the Retina, its first 35 mm camera, which also used film that was sold in a preloaded metal cassette.

1936 – Kodachrome color film is introduced for 35 mm slides and 8 mm home movies; the Argus Model A camera, the first mass produced 35 mm camera produced in the United States, is introduced.

1939 – Kodak introduced "Ready-Mount" cardboard mounts for 35 mm Kodachrome slides.

1942 – Kodacolor film for making color prints from a true color film negative is introduced by Kodak. Prints made from this film by Kodak often have a stamp on the reverse that includes the date of processing giving you a rough idea of when a photograph was taken. Keep in mind that the film may have been processed sometime after its exposure. Kodacolor prints will probably have experienced some changes in the color over time. This can be corrected through digital editing on a computer.

1948 – Polaroid Land camera, Model 95, went on sale in Boston, Massachusetts, on November 26, 1948 which produced a 3 ¼ x 4 ¼ in. sepia colored print that was deckle-edged.

1954 – Polaroid Model 80 Highlander introduced that made a 2 ¼ x 3 ¼ in. black-and - white print.

1963 – Polaroid Polacolor Land film was introduced that made a full-color print.

1971 – Polaroid Colorpack 80 camera is introduced that made an almost 3 ¼ in. square print.

1972 – Polaroid SX-70 Land camera that produced a 3 ½ x 4 ¼ in. print goes on sale. This print is developed outside of the camera in the sealed photograph packet.

Annotated Bibliography

The following resources can help in the research, care, collecting and purchase of African American photographs. Use **amazon.com** on the internet to purchase books that may not be available in your local library.

Berg, Paul. *Nineteenth Century Photographic Cases and Wall Frames*. Huntington Beach, CA: Huntington Valley Press, Second Edition, 2004. Berg has attempted with great success to document all of the designs used for the types of cases and frames that housed and displayed early images. A valuable rarity ranking and price guide is also included.

Burns, Stanley B. *Forgotten Marriage, The Painted Tintype & the Decorative Frame, 1860-1910*. New York, NY: The Burns Press, 1995. Burns gives a history of the tinted photography with a focus on the painted tintype along with an analysis of the frames used to display them. Discussion of frame styles can be particularly useful in dating framed tintypes and photographs.

Craig, John S. *Craig's Daguerreian Registry*. Torrington, CT: John Craig, 1994. www.daguerreotype.com This is a classic work invaluable for the dating of early photographs made before 1860 that are signed by the photographers. Covering the entire country, locations of photographers and their dates of operation are provided that are an invaluable help in the research of early images. Information can also be accessed through his website.

Darrah, William C. *The World of Stereographs*. Gettysburg, PA: William C. Darrah, 1977. Darrah's book is the classic history of stereography and a comprehensive study stereoviews and their publishers.

Davis, Keith. *George Barnard: Photographer of Sherman's Campaign*. Kansas City, MO: Hallmark Cards, Inc., 1990. The life and work photographer George Barnard receives deserved attention in this well illustrated biography that includes reproductions of his 1866 *Photographic Views of Sherman's Campaign*. Barnard's photographs of African Americans are also examined.

Gagel, Diane VanSkive. *Ohio Photographers, 1839-1900.* Nevada City, CA: Carl Mautz Publishing, 1998. This is the most complete reference work identifying early Ohio photographers that will help to date photographs taken there based on the time period of operation of photographers at specific locations.

Gladstone, William. *Men of Color.* Gettysburg PA: Thomas Publications, 1993. Gladstone's book investigates the roles that African Americans played in the Union Army during the Civil War. Artifacts from his comprehensive collection, including many photographs and the stories behind them, are used as illustrations.

Jezierski, John V. *Enterprising Images: The Goodridge Brothers, African American Photographers 1847-1922.* Detroit, MI: Wayne State University Press, 2000. This is the definitive study of the lives and work of the black photographer Glenalvin Goodridge and his brothers.

Kelbaugh, Ross J., *Directory of Civil War Photographers, Vol. One: Maryland Delaware, Washington, D.C., Northern Virginia, West Virginia.* Baltimore, MD: Historic Graphics, 1990.

Kelbaugh, Ross J. *Directory of Civil War Photographers, Vol. Two: Pennsylvania, New Jersey.* Baltimore, MD: Historic Graphics, 1991.

Kelbaugh, Ross J. *Directory of Civil War Photographers, Vol. Three: Western States and Territories.* Baltimore, MD: Historic Graphics, 1992. These are the first three volumes that compile listings of photographers active during the Civil War period that have been gathered from city directories and the Internal Revenue Assessment lists where photographers were required to obtain an annual license to operate. These resources help date the locations and periods of activity of specific studios which adds more critical information to interpreting Civil War period photographs. These are available for purchase from the author at **www.HistoricGraphics.com**.

Kelbaugh, Ross J. *Directory of Maryland Photographers, 1839-1900.* Baltimore, MD: Historic Graphics, 1989. Over 750 professional photographers are documented in this directory and the use of newspapers, directories, census records, and other resources have provided information as to the specific locations and time periods of their studio activity. This helps in the determining the specific period in which an image was made and is available from the author at **www.HistoricGraphics.com**.

Kelbaugh, Ross J. *An Introduction to Civil War Photography.* Gettysburg, PA: Thomas Publications, 1989. This modestly priced publication discusses the photography of the Civil War, the processes, the formats, and some of the stories about those that helped to create this extraordinary visual legacy. Useful advice for collecting is also included.

Krainik, Clifford & Michele. *Union Cases, A Collector's Guide to the Art of America's First Plastics.* Grantsburg, WI: Centennial Photo Service, 1988. This is the definitive work on the history of the union cases (sometimes incorrectly called "gutta percha" cases) used to house early images. A comprehensive collection of examples is also included along with a discussion of rarity.

Massengill, Stephen E., *Photographers in North Carolina, The First Century, 1842-1942.* Raleigh, NC: North Carolina Office of Archives and History, 2004. Massengil documents more than 2500 photographers active during the medium's first century in North Carolina. The Biographical Directory includes locations and dates of photographic activities for photographers which help to date signed photographs.

Reilly, James M. *Care Identification of 19th-Centurty Photographic Prints.* Rochester, NY: Eastman Kodak Co., 1986. This invaluable publication gives a technical look at all of the types of photographs produced in the 19th century, how they were made, how they can be identified and recommendations for preservation and conservation. It also includes a valuable wall chart the illustrates differences between various types of photographic reproductions from the era.

Ries, Linda and Jay W. Ruby. *Directory of Pennsylvania Photographers, 1839-1900*. [Harrisburg]: Pennsylvania Historical and Museum Commission, 1999. This is the most complete state-wide directory of Pennsylvania photographers of the nineteenth century and is invaluable for dating photographs with studio names.

Rinhart, Floyd and Marion. *The American Daguerreotype*. Athens, Georgia: The University of Georgia Press, 1981. The Rinhart's were pioneer collectors and researchers of early American photography. This book takes an in-depth look at the practice of daguerreotypy in the U.S.

Severa, Joan. *Dressed for the Photographer, Ordinary Americans & Fashion, 1840-1900*. Kent, OH: Kent State University Press, 1995. This book surveys changing fashions for men, women, and children during the era of 19th century photography providing another useful for dating photographs by clothing styles. Includes illustrations and analysis of some portraits of African Americans.

Shumard, Ann M. *A Durable Momento, Portraits by Augustus Washington, African American Daguerreotypist*. Washington, DC: National Portrait Gallery, 1999. Catalogue to accompany the traveling exhibit that investigates the career of African American daguerrean Augustus Washington. Illustrated with numerous color reproductions of his work including his portrait of John Brown and daguerreotypes he made in the American Colonization Society's settlement in Liberia, Africa.

Smith, Margaret Denton and Tucker, Mary Louise. *Photography in New Orleans, The Early Years, 1840-1865*. Baton Rouge, LA: Louisiana State University Press, 1982. Scholarly study of photography's early years in New Orleans which includes a useful directory of New Orleans photographers. The career of black photographer Jules Lion is examined in depth.

Sullivan, George. *Black Artists in Photography, 1840-1940*. New York, NY: Cobblehill Books, 1996. Sullivan's presents short biographies of black photographers that include Jules Lion, Augustus Washington, James P. Ball, the Goodridge Brothers, Cornelius M. Battey, and Addison Scurlock.

Steele, Chris and Polito, Ronald. *A Directory of Massachusetts Photographers, 1839-1900*. Camden, ME: Picton Press, 1993. This is the primary reference for determining the location and period of activity for 19th century Massachusetts photographers and helps in the dating of images from their studios.

Taft, Robert. *Photography and the American Scene*. New York: Dover, 1964 (reprint of the 1938 edition). Taft's work is the classic history of 19th century photography in the U.S.

Teal, Harvey S. *Partners with the Sun: South Carolina Photographers, 1840-1940*. Columbia, SC: Univ. of South Carolina Press, 2001. Teal's work represents the kind of regional photographic histories that need to be written before another general history of the medium in the United States is attempted. This book is particularly valuable in regards to photography as it was practiced in this state during the Civil War. Information is included that will help in the dating of photographs signed by South Carolina photographers.

Waldsmith, John. *Stereo Views: An Illustrated History and Price Guide*. Iola, WI: Krause Publications, 1991. This is a general guide to the history and collecting of 19th and early 20th century stereoviews. A comprehensive price guide is included which can help indicate the most valuable views even if the prices are out of date.

Willis, Deborah. *Black Photographers, 1840-1940: An Illustrated Bio-Bibliography*. New York: Garland Publishing, 1985.

Willis, Deborah. *Black Photographers, 1940-1980: An Illustrated Bio-Bibliography*. New York: Garland Publishing, 1989. These two landmark books provide a directory and biographical information of select African American photographers, along with public exhibits, selected bibliography and samples of their work covering 1840 to 1988.

Willis, Deborah. *J.P. Ball, Daguerrean and Studio Photographer*. New York: Garland Publishing, Inc., 1993. This is the first book to examine the life of James P. Ball and present a comprehensive collection of his photographs.

Willis-Braithwaite, Deborah. *VanDerZee, Photographer 1886-1983*. New York: Harry N. Abrams, Inc., 1993. Published as a catalogue to accompany an exhibit of the same name at the National Portrait Gallery in Washington, D.C., this book reviews the life and work and a legendary African American photographer whose work continues to increase in demand among collectors.

Wilson, Jackie N. *Hidden Witness, African-American Images from the Dawn of Photography to the Civil War*. New York: St. Martin's Press,1999. This is a catalogue of the cased image collection of African Americans assembled by Jackie N. Wilson along with examples from the J. Paul Getty Museum.

Preservation Supplies/Archival Sleeves

Gaylord
Library Supplies, Furniture, Archival Solutions
www.gaylord.com

Light Impressions
P.O. Box 787, Brea, CA 92822
1-800-828-6216
www.lightimpressionsdirect.com

Rusty Norton
P.O. Box 1070, New Haven, CT 06504
203-281-0066
www.tecsolv.com/stereoview/home.html

Carl Mautz
Vintage Photographs
228 Commercial St. #522, Nevada City, CA 95959
916-478-1610
www.nccn.net/~cmautz/

University Products
517 Main St., Box 101, Holyoke, MA 01041
www.universityproducts.com

Photograph Conservation

American Institute for Conservation of Historic & Artistic Works
1717 K Street, NW, Suite 200, Washington, DC 20006
aic.stanford.edu

The AIC is a professional membership organization that supports programs and publications concerning conservation issues. Their website also maintains a list of professional conservators who specialize in photographs.

Library of Congress
lcweb.loc.gov/preserv/care/photolea.html

This is a useful leaflet covering the care, handling, and storage of old photographs.

National Park Service Conserv O Grams
www.cr.nps.gov/museum/publications/conserveogram/conserv.html

The NPS posts for downloading the latest research and advice for care and display of historical artifacts. Though aimed at NPS personnel, many useful articles about the care of photographs are included that can help anyone.

Northeast Document Conservation Center
100 Brickstone Square, Andover, MA 01810-1494
(978) 475-6021
www.nedcc.org

This is a non-profit organization that provides solutions to conservation problems relating to paper and photographs for libraries, archives, museums as well as for individuals.

Wilhelm Imaging Research
www.wilhelm-research.com

With the increased move towards the use of inkjet and other digital printers for photograph duplication, questions arise about how long they will last. This group tests the latest equipment and shares the results. Many other informative articles related to photo preservation are also posted.

Photography Collector Organizations

The following organizations include members that collect and deal in African American images. They also publish membership rosters, newsletters, magazines and journals. All hold annual meetings which include trade fairs where African American images can be bought and sold. Their websites include links to photography dealers and resources for supplies.

The Daguerreian Society
3043 West Liberty Ave., Pittsburgh, Pa. 15216-2460
www.daguerre.org

National Stereoscopic Association, Inc.
P.O. Box 86708, Portland, OR 97286
www.stereoview.org

Photographic Historical Society of New England
www.phsne.org

The PHSNE meets on a monthly basis and sponsors a spring and fall photographica show. They also publish a quarterly journal for members.

Auctions featuring African American Photographs

The following conduct periodic catalogue and online auctions that include African American material.

Alexander Autographs
100 Melrose Ave., Suite 100, Greenwich, CT 06830
www.alexautographs.com

Christie's Auction House
www.Christies.com

Christie's hold several photography auctions every year at their various international galleries.

Cowan's Auctions, Inc.
673 Wilmer Ave., Cincinnati, OH 45226
www.cowanauctions.com

Wes Cowan, familiar to many through his appearances on the Antique Roadshow, holds several catalogue/internet auctions a year that often include important vintage black photographs.

Early American History Auctions, Inc.
P.O. Box 3507, Rancho Santa Fe, CA 92067
www.earlyamerican.com

Ebay
www.ebay.com

Collectibles>Cultures,Ethnicities>Black Americana>Photos
Collectibles>Photographic Images
Collectibles>Photographic Images>Antique(pre-1940)>Daguerreotypes
Collectibles>Photographic Images>Antique(pre-1940)>Ambrotypes
Collectibles>Photographic Images>Antique(pre-1940)>CDVs
Collectibles>Photographic Images>Antique(pre-1940)>Cabinet Photos
Collectibles>Photographic Images>Antique(pre-1940)>Tintypes
Collectibles>Photographic Images>Antique(pre-1940)>Stereoviews
Collectibles>Postcards & Paper>Postcards>Real Photo
Collectibles>Militia>Civil War (1861-65)>Original Period Items

On eBay you will find the greatest quantity of collectible black photographs offered for sale anywhere ranging from daguerreotypes to modern gelatin silver prints. Listed are some of the categories in which they may be found.

Larry Gottheim BE-HOLD, Inc.
78 Rockland Ave., Yonkers, NY 10705
www.be-hold.com

Internet and print catalogue auctions of vintage photograph held several times a year usually include black subject images.

Payle's Online Auctions
www.playle.com

Internet auction site where dealers list postcards, ephemera, and collectibles. Site includes useful information for dating photo postcards.

Raynor's Historical Collectible Auctions
24 NW Court Square, Suite 201, Graham, NC 27253
www.hcaauctions.com

Raynor's holds several absentee catalogue auctions every year that include black Americana. Bids can be submitted by phone, fax, or online.

Sotheby's
http://search.sothebys.com/

Sotheby's holds at least two catalogue auctions for photographs in New York every year. Higher quality material featuring photographs of and by African Americans will be found among their sales. Be sure to check their international auctions as well. Sales can be viewed online.

Swann's Auction Galleries
104 East 25th St., New York, NY 10010
www.swanngalleries.com

Swann's holds a specialized auction of African American material every February during Black History Month. Black photographs can be found in their specialized photography sale held several times a year.

Where to see African American Photographs

George Eastman House/ International Museum of Photography and Film
900 East Ave., Rochester, NY 14607
www.eastmanhouse.org

The GEH/IMP located at the home of George Eastman, founder of Kodak, is a museum and educational institution focusing on the history of photography and motion pictures. Their collection includes African-American photographs and their website features selections of these images.

Library of Congress
www.loc.gov

The Library of Congress maintains a huge number of digital photographs, including many of African Americans, available online as part of the "American Memory" collections, online exhibits, and digital collections for researchers. From the site's homepage, do a search for "image lists" to find the extensive research collections.

Reginald F. Lewis Museum of Maryland African American History and Culture
830 East Pratt St., Baltimore, MD 21202
www.AfricanAmericanCulture.org

The museum opening in 2005 is dedicated to collecting, preserving,, interpreting, documenting and exhibiting the contributions of African Americans throughout Maryland's history.

Schomburg Center for Research in Black Culture
515 Malcolm X Blvd., New York, NY 10037-1801
(212) 491-2200
www.nypl.org (New York Public Library)

The extensive photograph collections of the Schomburg Center, which is part of the New York Public Library, can be searched through an online catalogue and selections can be viewed through online exhibits on their website and by visiting their research center.

Charles H. Wright Museum of African American History
315 E. Warren Ave., Detroit, MI 48201-1443
www.maah-detroit.org

This is currently the largerst African American history museum in the United States. Its exhibitions feature many historical and contemporary photographs.

Genealogy Research Internet Sites

The internet is revolutionizing genealogical research as more and more information is made available online. **Be sure to check with your local public library to see if they offer free access to any of the fee based genealogy sites!**

AfriGeneas.com

This is a comprehensive website for anyone interested in African American genealogy. It has many helpful guides for conducting research online, as well as several free data bases. These include lists of blacks living in Baltimore 1810-1866, a searchable database of surnames, and the "Slave Data Collection" which includes the names of slaves extracted from the records of slaveholders. It also includes a chat room for exchanging information.

Afro-American Historical and Genealogical Society, Inc.
www.AAHGS.org

This is a national organization for those researching black genealogy that sponsors conferences, and publishes a bimonthly newsletter and semiannual journal. The website also lists local AAHGS chapters of genealogists.

Ancestry.com

This website has one of the largest number of data bases that can be searched online for genealogical information. Several levels of monthly or annual membership fees determine which records you can access.

Civil War Soldiers & Sailors System
www.civilwar.nps.gov/cwss

This National Park Service provides free access to the basic records of Civil War service men along with regimental histories and other related data bases. Some are incomplete at this time, but it a good place to begin a search. This site also links to the searchable database of information relating to African American sailors.

Familysearch.org

The Church of Jesus Christ of Latter-day Saints (Mormons) provides free access to a large number of genealogical records both online and at their Family History Center around the country. The 1880 U.S. Census is one of several databases that are available online.

Genealogy.com

This site offers several levels of membership which determine which databases can be used. Access to census records are available at the highest level.

Heritagequestonline.com

Databases and other genealogical resources are provided though this website for access from public libraries. Access to many census records are variable. Check with your local public library to see if they are members of this site.

The Price Guide for African American Photographs

For a current listing of actual prices paid at auctions and shows for African American photographs, visit the author's website (www.HistoricGraphics.com).

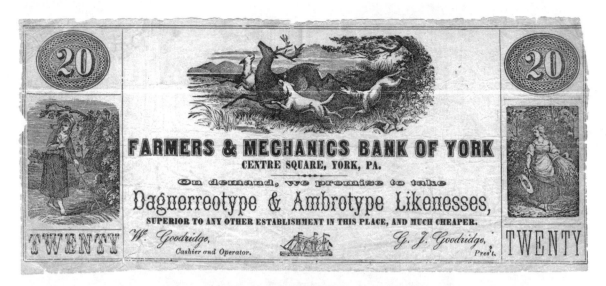

This advertisement for the African American owned photography gallery of Glenalvin Goodridge in York, Pennsylvania, was designed to resemble an actual banknote at a time when banks could issue their own paper currency.

ABOUT THE AUTHOR

Ross J. Kelbaugh's interest in early photography was started while he was still in elementary school at the beginning of the Civil War Centennial celebrations in the early 1960s. He soon acquired his first photographs of Union and Confederate soldiers as part of his general collecting of relics from the period. After graduating from college in 1971, he expanded his collecting to focus on 19th and 20th century American photographs and he acquired many of the images that are published here for the first time.

Mr. Kelbaugh was awarded a BA from the University of Maryland, College Park and a MLA from Johns Hopkins University. His first career was teaching American history, archaeology, and Advanced Placement American Government at Catonsville High School in Baltimore County before retiring in 2001. In recognition of his contributions to the field, he was selected as "Teacher-Historian" by the United States Capitol Historical Society in Washington, D.C.

Today he heads Historic Graphics, LLC, a vintage image solutions company that has provided period paintings, prints, and photographs for interior sets of the Turner Motion Pictures Civil War movie "Gods and Generals" as well as images and artifacts for the Reginald Lewis Museum of Maryland African-American History and Culture in Baltimore, Maryland. He continues to specialize in collecting, researching and lecturing on 19th century Maryland photography as part of his general interest in early American images. Mr. Kelbaugh's publications include the *Directory of Maryland Photographers, 1839-1900*, the first reference work ever published on this state's photographic industry; *Introduction to Civil War Photography*; and the multi-volume series *Directory of Civil War Photographers*. Mr. Kelbaugh can be contacted through his website at www.HistoricGraphics.com.

The Little Cowboy, gelatin silver print ca. 1950.

Prints suitable for framing of most photographs in this book are available for purchase. Please visit www.HistoricGraphics.com for ordering information.

THOMAS PUBLICATIONS publishes books about the American Colonial era, the Revolutionary War, the Civil War, and other important topics. For a complete list of titles, please visit our website at:

www.thomaspublications.com

Or write to:

THOMAS PUBLICATIONS
P.O. Box 3031
Gettysburg, Pa. 17325